DISASTER HEROES
Invisible Champions of
Help, Hope, and Healing

by
Suzanne Bernier

with

Candice L. Davis

Disaster Heroes

Copyright © 2015 Suzanne Bernier

Published 2015.

First published by Faith Books & MORE

ISBN 978-1-939761-32-3

Printed in the United States of America

This book is printed on acid-free paper.

 3255 Lawrenceville-Suwanee Rd. | Suite P250
Suwanee, GA 30024
publishing@faithbooksandmore.com
faithbooksandmore.com

Ordering Information:

Quantity sales. Special discounts are available on quantity purchases by corporations, associations, and others. For details, contact the publisher at the address above.

Orders by U.S. trade bookstores and wholesalers. Please contact Ingram Book Company: Tel: (800) 937-8000; Email: orders@ingrambook.com or visit ipage.ingrambook.com.

This book is dedicated to my very first hero and mentor, Raoul Peter Boire. Without his guidance, tutelage, faith in me, and support throughout the most crucial years of my life, I would not be who or where I am today. If every high school teacher and guidance counselor were more like him, the world would truly be a better place. xo

"When I was a boy and I would see scary things in the news, my mother would say to me, 'Look for the helpers. You will always find people who are helping.' To this day, especially in times of "disaster," I remember my mother's words, and I am always comforted by realizing that there are still so many helpers — so many caring people in this world." — Fred Rogers (Mr. Rogers)

Acknowledgements

While there are far too many people to individually recognize for their contributions, either direct or indirect, in the development of this book, there are a few I must single out: The Honorable Tom Ridge, Candice L. Davis, Bob Nakao, Marty Plevel, Yumiko Kiuchi, Akiko Inouye, Jennifer Gallagher, Nicole Antoinette Smith, Sim Wong, Kimberly Best, Karina Pillay Kinnee, Vanessa Bjornson, Michelle Short, David Burton, The Japan Foundation of Toronto, Clyde and Lorraine Berger, Jock Menzies, Justin Butts, Graham Kent, Shannon Toomey, and Dillon Richard.

And of course, a huge thank you to all the heroes who agreed to meet with me and share their inspiring stories and photos.

Table of Contents

Foreword

"The ultimate measure of a man is not where he stands in moments of comfort and convenience, but where he stands at times of challenge and controversy."
-Martin Luther King Jr.

On September 11, 2001, most Americans concluded, as I did, that we had seen the worst of humanity. Yet, a quick trip through history, would remind us that, as a species, we can wreak - and have often wrought -unspeakable pain and suffering upon one another. As recently as the concentration camps of World War II to the events of 9/11, the Boston Marathon, the global scourge of radical terrorists, the grim realities of humanity's darker capabilities have been proven time and again.

But humans also have a tremendous capacity for compassion; a sense of unity so powerful it trumps race, gender, religion, nationality, and even our own egos. We have an innate ability to focus squarely on what's important in times of need - a beautiful faculty to see anyone as our own brother or sister - and go out of our way to help ease the suffering of others.

We often don't hear about these people or their acts because recognition isn't their goal - they do it purely out of the good of their heart, and they're happy to carry on without a parade. It is, after all, the golden rule: to do unto others as you would have them do unto you. And while it can sometimes seem as though these people are few and far between, I can assure you first-hand that they are not. They are only silent heroes.

I do, however, believe that these people deserve to be recognized for their actions. Not because the act needs reward, but because it deserves publicity. People deserve to know that there are courageous men and women out there who are doing what they can in critical moments to help victims of tragedy. They deserve to be inspired by others to do likewise. And these selfless acts of solidarity are just as telling of the depths of our humanitarianism as our embarrassing missteps are telling of the extremes of our emotions.

Suzanne Bernier has compiled a moving selection of stories from philanthropic men and women around the globe who acted with compassion and love in the face of catastrophe, be it natural or man-made. They didn't just talk about what should be done; they did it. They helped rescue, rebuild, and restore a faith in humanity that, especially in the face of such misfortune, can at times seem a foregone idea.

We often ask ourselves, what evil, or demons, exist in the hearts of individuals that drives such inhumanity. There is no conceivable way we can possibly understand or comprehend such depravity. Yet, at the same time, as we relate to the people and stories in this book, there is no confusion as to what motivates selfless people to do the right thing, the compassionate and caring thing. It is clearly the "better angels" of their nature and of humankind. These inspirational stories give us both hope and cause for celebration.

The Honorable Tom Ridge,

First Secretary of the U.S. Department of Homeland Security

Introduction

The late Fred Rogers, beloved and gentle host of PBS's Mister Rogers' Neighborhood for over thirty years, once said, "When I was a boy and I would see scary things in the news, my mother would say to me, 'Look for the helpers. You will always find people who are helping.' To this day, especially in times of disaster, I remember my mother's words and I am always comforted by realizing that there are still so many helpers—so many caring people in this world."

Indeed, helpers and heroes are everywhere, and they shine brightest in darkness.

I became inspired to write this book following my first "voluntourist" effort in New Orleans, about eighteen months post-Katrina. As much of the media coverage had long since died down by then, I had no idea how bad it still was—until I started hearing about and meeting the countless survivors, first responders, and volunteers who were helping to rebuild and recover the city of New Orleans. That's when I decided I wanted to share the stories of these helpers with the rest of the world.

This book is in no way meant to downplay the tragic losses and devastation experienced following disasters, but rather to share some of the life-affirming stories of help and heroism that shine through.

Everyone remembers that fateful morning of September 11, 2001 in New York City following the terror attacks on the World Trade Center. That day changed us all forever. Within the emergency management community, it redefined us and introduced us to the violent reality of terrorism.

However, the events of that day also brought out the best in people. I remember seeing televised images of thousands of strangers silently walking together, supporting one another, holding each other up. Ordinary citizens stepped in to help direct traffic and carry the wounded.

There were countless stories of people throughout Manhattan, New York, and New Jersey taking in strangers who couldn't get home that night. Condolences and messages of support came in from all over the world. The horrific events of that day united us all.

These and other actions on 9/11 and in the days, months, and years that followed are beautiful examples of our basic human instinct to support and help others in need following a disaster or life-threatening event.

Courageous and dedicated men and women risk their lives daily to ensure our safety. Police, fire, EMS, and other emergency response organizations perform acts of heroism every single day. These men and women are true examples of heroism and are hopefully recognized regularly for their efforts, as they should be. But there are many other heroes most people don't ever hear about.

After every disaster, we are bombarded with images of death, devastation, and destruction. The media rarely focuses on the countless helpers behind the scenes. In the chapters that follow, you will read the inspiring stories of everyday people, from all walks of life, who have helped communities respond, recover, and rebuild following some of the world's largest disasters, from 9/11 onward. While these events reveal our fragility, they also demonstrate how resilient we humans really are and highlight our natural urge to come together during times of crisis to help our neighbors.

When I started meeting and interviewing the people profiled in this book, I realized they all shared similar characteristics. Empathy, selflessness, and perseverance were three common traits in all the disaster heroes I met, as well as creativity, initiative, and "thinking outside the box." I also discovered heroism can be demonstrated in many different forms and is displayed every day by men, women, girls, and boys of all ages and backgrounds.

All of the stories had another thing in common. They each

demonstrated how just one person with one idea could snowball into an effort involving hundreds, if not thousands, of others who donated their time, money, and efforts to help disaster survivors.

As we enter a new era of emergency management, I hope communities continue to recognize the need for collaboration between first responders, practitioners, and everyday volunteers after a disaster. By doing so, we can become more creative, innovative, and respectful of the roles, ideas, and experiences we all bring to the table during a crisis.

Hockey legend Wayne Gretzky once said, "You miss 100% of the shots you don't take." The stories in this book recount the tales of ordinary people who took a shot and made a bigger impact on people's lives than they could have ever imagined.

I hope you enjoy reading their stories as much as I enjoyed documenting them.

Ronnie Goldman

The 9/11 Terror Attacks

The Spirit of Louisiana

Eighteen months after Hurricane Katrina ravaged New Orleans and much of the Gulf Coast, I spoke at a disaster conference in NOLA. It was my first visit to New Orleans, and it was during this trip that I met the hero who planted the seed for this book, Ronnie Goldman.

The conference organizer, Bob Nakao, had asked the speakers if we would be willing to stay behind and donate a couple of extra days to local rebuilding projects. Of course I jumped at the opportunity, and it ended up being one of the best and most important decisions of my life.

At the time of this writing, Bob's volunteer initiative Continuity Cares, persists in its good work, and many of us meet annually to help rebuild fire stations, schools, homes, and other critical infrastructure across the United States.

With Bob Nakao, the creator of Continuity Cares, at our first rebuilding effort, a fire station in New Orleans. Photo credit: Mary Parrish

Marty Plevel and Ronnie Goldman (left to right) the first day we met rebuilding a New Orleans fire station in April 2007. Photo credit: Suzanne Bernier

My first Continuity Cares project, in April 2007, brought us all together for the rebuilding of the inside of a New Orleans fire station badly damaged by Katrina. This particular station was one of the last in the area to be rebuilt. I was assigned to a team made up of conference speakers and local volunteers, and I quickly connected with two friendly and delightful men who appeared to be great life-long friends. They were Ronnie Goldman, from New Orleans, and Marty Plevel, from New York City. Little did I know one would become the inspiration for my first book, and both would become two of my dearest friends and colleagues.

Together, Marty and Ronnie proceeded to tell me the story of the Spirit of Louisiana, and I learned that Ronnie, a local telephone engineer, started a state-wide fundraising campaign after watching President Bush address the nation while standing atop one of the thirty-five fire trucks destroyed in the September 11, 2001 terror attacks.

This is the story of Ronnie and the Spirit of Louisiana, the story that prompted me to become an author so I could share it with the readers of this book. Thank you, Ronnie, for letting me share your uplifting story with the rest of the world, and for being a true disaster hero and friend.

New Orleans native Ronnie Goldman considers himself an average person, just a regular guy. But few regular guys ever commit such a great act of generosity it brings groups of the toughest men to tears of appreciation. Millions of average people walk through Times Square every day for years and never get stopped by strangers who recognize them and feel compelled to thank them for what they've done for the city of New York. Rare is the citizen who starts a movement that creates an enduring bond between two of the country's most beloved cities.

On September 14, 2001, Ronnie was making coleslaw in the kitchen of his Louisiana home, when he heard the voice of President George W. Bush. In the early aftermath of 9/11, any news surrounding the tragedy drew the Goldmans, like most Americans, to the television, and Ronnie set down his knife to join his wife, Sandie, in watching the short speech by the nation's leader.

It was a bleak scene. An American flag flew from the arm of a street lamp. On one side of the tableau, intact skyscrapers gleamed in the sun, testaments to the prosperity of New York City's financial district, in contrast to the building on the other side, which, though still standing, offered broken windows and twisted steel as evidence of the recent terrorist attacks. Suspending their work to listen to the president, men in hard hats positioned themselves on and around debris from the fallen towers.

In the middle of it all, President Bush stood atop a pile of rubble. Next to him was a veteran firefighter dressed in jeans, a sweatshirt with the FDNY emblem (the acronym a nod to the historic name of the city's fire department), and a firefighter's helmet; a pair of goggles and a respirator mask hung around his neck. President Bush embraced the firefighter with one arm and took up a bullhorn to address the assembly of World Trade Center rescue and recovery workers.

"I want you all to know," said the president, "this nation stands with the good people of New York City, and New Jersey, and Connecticut, as we mourn the loss of thousands of our citizens." After some impassioned banter with the crowd, the two-minute speech came to a close, the workers on the scene chanting, "USA! USA! USA!" as President Bush departed.

As the camera pulled back for a wide shot, Ronnie Goldman realized the makeshift platform from which the president had spoken wasn't just wreckage from the destroyed buildings. It was, in fact, a burned out fire truck. The news that the fire department had lost ninety-eight vehicles, ranging from ladder trucks and hazmat vehicles to ambulances and sedans, hadn't gotten much coverage in the wake of so many lost lives. Seeing the destroyed truck, Ronnie told his wife, "New York is in deep trouble. We've got to start a drive right now to show these terrorists who they're playing with. And we're going to rebuild the New York Fire Department."

He had not an inkling of the life-changing events he'd set in motion with that proclamation. Ronnie confesses he only said it in the emotion of the moment, but Sandie, called him on his big talk. She suggested that, as the one who came up with the idea, Ronnie should take on the task of seeing it through to fruition.

Once he wrapped his mind around the notion that he could launch the initiative himself, Ronnie figured he should reach out to someone with the power and influence to ignite a statewide effort. "Live Mike," a weekly radio show hosted by David Tyree, provided an opportunity for constituents to talk one-on-one with Louisiana's governor, Mike Foster, and Ronnie figured the show could serve as his direct line to the top of the state's government.

What he had in mind was no small feat. Ronnie planned to suggest that Louisiana, one of the poorest states in the Union, should help finance the rebuilding of the New York City Fire Department. Rather than blindside the governor on-air with a proposal he might find ludicrous, Ronnie ran the idea of building a new fire truck for the FDNY by David Tyree first, suggesting that the governor challenge other states to join Louisiana in their commitment to sending aid.

To Ronnie Goldman's surprise, David loved the idea, and he promised to get Ronnie on air to speak with the governor. David was as good as his word, and the next day, Ronnie found himself engaged in a lengthy and enthusiastic discussion with Governor Foster. By the end of the conversation, it was clear that Ronnie's impulse to do something for the people of New York had evolved into a mission that had the governor's attention and support.

In a stroke of good fortune of the sort that would happen again and again over the course of the project, Chris Ferrara heard the broadcast, and he called the governor at home that night. Ronnie recounts that Chris, the owner of Ferrara Fire Apparatus, told the governor, "We're building this truck. Furthermore, we're going to have it ready for Christmas."

A question remained: Was it permissible to spend state funds to build an emergency vehicle that wouldn't serve the people of Louisiana? With the approval of the State Attorney General, a small committee took a measure before the Louisiana State Legislature. It passed unanimously, a first in the history of the legislative body, granting permission for state funds to be accessed for the project. Still, Hunt Downer, Speaker of the Louisiana House, had an idea that would make the venture more personal for Louisianans. He proposed that they take it to the people of the state and allow them to contribute through private donations. Apparently, the other state legislators agreed. Before the day ended, they'd donated over $17,000 of their own money to the cause.

Thus was born the "Bucks for Trucks" campaign, with the people of Louisiana backing it from its inception. Schoolchildren collected pennies, held fundraisers, and sent in their lunch money. Local schools challenged each other to see which institution could raise the most money, and police departments competed with fire departments to see which could give more. Grocery stores solicited donations from customers as they checked out. A woman living in a retirement home sent $100 along with a letter of apology. She was on a fixed income, she said, and she was sorry she didn't have more to give. The money poured in. When Fire Chief Gerald Dellucky, who served as treasurer, made the first deposit for the fund, it totaled $38,000. In the end, the generosity of the people of Louisiana would make it unnecessary to dip into the state coffers to build the fire truck.

During those early weeks, few people knew the identity of the caller who'd reached out to the governor on air, and Ronnie Goldman was perfectly content for his participation to remain anonymous. In fact, when he was invited to visit the manufacturer in Holden, Louisiana, for the November 7th christening of the truck's chassis, he expected to get in and out of the event without much fanfare. "I figured me and the governor were going to break a bottle of Bud over the bumper, and that's it," Ron says. "I had no idea what I was getting into."

The governor arrived by helicopter, and Marsanne Golsby, his press secretary, steered Ronnie and Sandie over to meet Governor Foster and his wife in person, but once the ceremony started, Ronnie slipped to the back of the crowd. When Fire Chief Butch Browning called Ronnie Goldman up to be recognized, Ronnie was caught off guard. He'd seriously underestimated the grandness of the event and the part organizers expected him to play in it. "I didn't even have a coat and tie on," he recalls.

With local and national media outlets on hand, the anonymity Ronnie had enjoyed so far came to an end, as the cameras and microphones were turned in his direction. Realizing they had the man who'd started it all in their midst, employees at Ferrara Fire Apparatus applauded him and came over to shake his hand. "I really felt out of place," Ronnie says of all the attention.

He'd have to get used to it. Later that month, as he drove in heavy traffic, Ronnie received a call from the radio station that would perpetuate and extend his celebrity. David Tyree wanted to talk to him on the air again, so Ronnie pulled into a parking lot to take the call. "It's a good thing I did," Ronnie explains. "I'd have wrecked the car." On live radio, David passed on a message to Ronnie from Governor Foster. He wanted to take the Goldmans with him to present the truck to the people of New York City. Ronnie called Sandie. "Pack your drawers," he told her. "We're going to New York to bring them this fire truck."

Although eager to witness firsthand the moment when New York City firefighters received the truck, Ronnie felt uneasy about taxpayers financing his trip. He needn't have worried. Avaya, the company where Ronnie worked as a communications systems engineer, stepped in to make its contribution to the venture. His employer covered all the travel expenses for Ronnie, his wife, and their daughter, Krissy, to travel to New York City and participate in the hand-off of the truck to the FDNY.

The trip was all set when an executive from Ferrara Fire Apparatus revised the itinerary. He needed everyone to depart a day earlier. The group of Louisianans responsible for building the truck, including Governor Foster and Speaker Downer, Ronnie and his family, and representatives from Ferrara, had another stop to make. Before it reached its final destination, the new fire truck and its traveling companions would be received by President Bush at the White House.

With double-shifts, volunteer overtime labor, and manufacturers' contributions, the truck rolled off the line in just 45 days and at half the normal cost. By mid-December, the Spirit of Louisiana was ready for action. On December 17, 2001, the new fire truck drove into the Superdome during Monday Night Football, and Ronnie laid eyes on the final product of his impulsive act of beneficence, for the first time. After the game, the Goldmans flew to New York, and the Spirit and its small convoy departed for Washington, D.C., escorted by law enforcement vehicles from Mississippi and Louisiana.

Crossing into Mississippi, the New York-bound fire truck received an unexpected reception. Sparklers and flares lit up the night, and fire trucks and emergency vehicles lined the route.

As the Spirit of Louisiana passed by, the vehicles saluted with horn honks and flashing lights. One by one, trucks filled with firefighters and their families joined the convoy, extending it to more than three-quarters of a mile long. The display so moved Dean Smith, a fire department chaplain and Ferrara Fire Apparatus employee who volunteered his time to drive the truck to New York, that he had to pull the Spirit into a parking lot until the wave of emotion passed. "He had tears just running down his face," Ronnie says. "Mississippi just outdid themselves with that salute." The truck received a police escort in each state it crossed.

The Goldmans' party arrived in Washington via train on December 19th. "I had on a Winnie the Pooh tie," Ronnie recalls.

"Well, all I know is by the time we got to the train station that came off real fast. I was so, so wanting to go visit the president in my Winnie the Pooh tie." With Ronnie appropriately garbed in a tie decorated with American flags, the group loaded into the cab of the fire truck. Dean pointed out two floor pedals to Ronnie, who recounts, "I looked down and one says siren and one says horn, and I said 'Say no more.'" I blew that siren and that horn all the way to the White House." Escorted by D.C. motorcycle policemen, Georgetown police officers, and law enforcement cars from surrounding states, they quickly arrived at their destination.

After a detailed inspection of the truck by the Secret Service, the group was admitted to the White House and taken on an official tour, but Ronnie was diverted by a member of the President's staff. "This girl comes walking across Dolly Madison's carpet, and she raised the rope, and she said, 'Mr. Goldman, would you come with me please? The president is waiting.'"

The staff member led Ronnie to a room with a table and four chairs, two of which were occupied by Speaker Downer and Governor Foster. While Ronnie took a seat, the press corps and Louisiana's two senators stood to one side. "I'm sitting down, and I'm saying, 'What's wrong with this picture?'" recalls Ronnie.

Entering with his Secret Service contingent, President Bush joined the men at the table and welcomed them all to the White House. They talked for a few minutes, but when Mr. Bush asked Ronnie how he came up with the idea to build the truck, Ronnie's answer took the president aback. Ronnie explained that the president's brief speech at ground zero had inspired their effort to rebuild the New York City Fire Department.

Ronnie Goldman in The Spirit of Louisiana in the New Orleans Superdome during Monday Night Football on Dec 17, 2001, before leaving for Washington and New York. Photo credit: Krissy Cook

Ronnie Goldman in "The Spirit 2", a special operations unit delivered to New York on Jan 3,2003. Photo credit: Krissy Cook

Ronnie Goldman, his wife Sandie and their daughter Krissy in front of "The Spirit 2", a special operations unit delivered to New York on Jan 3,2003.

"Do you remember what you were standing on?" Ronnie asked, and the president said he did. He remembered it was a pile of rubble.

"I shook my head, and I pointed my finger, and I said, 'No, sir, Mr. President.' I said, 'You were standing on a burned out fire truck.'" Ronnie filled in the rest of the Spirit of Louisiana origin story, while Governor Foster and Speaker Downer listened. The meeting with the president, a surreal experience for Ronnie, came to an end when Press Secretary Ari Fleisher directed the group to the South Lawn for a press conference, during which President Bush praised Ronnie. "I particularly love this story, about how Ronnie decides to do something on behalf of the fellow citizens," the president said. "So he gets on the phone and calls a local radio personality—the governor.

And out of that came a huge volunteer effort in the State of Louisiana to provide help and aid to the good people of New York City. And I think Americans need to understand that this is the kind of story that makes our country so unique and so different. It's a story that makes me so proud to be the President of such a great, such a great land."

What followed was a whirlwind of kudos and expressions of gratitude, with Ronnie Goldman hailed as an American hero and President Bush visibly moved by emotion as he greeted a group of Louisiana firefighters and viewed the truck. The drama of the day took a comical twist when the group of Louisianans departed, somehow leaving Ronnie and Governor Foster behind at the White House. Between the Secret Service and the National Guard, that little misstep was efficiently rectified. The two men actually beat the rest of their party to New York, though Sandie insists that's because the two national guardsmen driving the vans got lost and refused to ask for directions.

Excitement surrounding the arrival of the Spirit of Louisiana only grew when Chris Ferrara, Ronnie Goldman, and others in their group officially turned the truck over to the New York City Fire Department on the Today show and were interviewed by Matt Lauer and Katie

Couric. Later that day, the visit turned somber when Ronnie and his companions made their way to ground zero, where more bodies had been recovered and victims' families were on site. The Louisianans decided to wait in their van, rather than trespass on such solemn circumstances. When Speaker Downer stuck his head in the van to see how everyone was doing, Ronnie blurted out, "Hunt, we don't belong here." Everyone agreed that it felt like a violation, as if they'd wandered onto sacred ground, and they hastily departed.

The Spirit of Louisiana was bound for Engine House 283, in the New York City borough of Brooklyn, and the Goldmans' group met Governor Foster and New York Governor George Pataki there for the delivery of the fire truck. Another crew from Louisiana had stepped in to cook a big pot of jambalaya for everyone, and a festive, yet reflective mood prevailed. Tears of gratitude mingled with tears of grief as the New York City firefighters thanked the Louisianans for their thoughtful generosity and shared memories of their fallen brothers.

Later, the New Yorkers invited their guests to the company Christmas party and took them caroling at fire stations around the city. At the firefighters' requests, Ronnie left his autograph on logbooks and fire trucks all along the way. As they crossed through Times Square, a random stranger tapped him on the shoulder to say thanks. New Yorkers recognized him from the news, and in the city's restaurants, Ronnie discovered his money was no good.

While Ronnie marveled at what he saw as his "undeserved celebrity," that fame was tied to the profound losses so many of the people they met had suffered. One such encounter stands out to Ronnie as he recalls the trip. As the father of three children, he empathized deeply with parents who lost sons and daughters on September 11th of that year. Meeting John Morello, a retired battalion chief and the father of fallen firefighter Vincent Morello, Ronnie shared with the man that he understood all too well what John was going through.

Ronnie Goldman at the White House with State Representative Hunt Downer, Louisiana Governor Mike Foster and President George W. Bush. Photo credit: Krissy Cook

Ronnie Goldman and "The Spirit of Louisiana" at the White House with State Representative Hunt Downer, Louisiana Governor Mike Foster and President George W. Bush. Photo credit: Krissy Cook

In 1990, at the age of sixteen, the Goldmans' son Tim succumbed to the leukemia he'd fought for half of his young life. Ronnie says of that moment with Mr. Morello, "He just looked at me, and we knew we had both experienced the same loss."

In an interview that night, Ronnie's daughter explained the practical magic that brought the Spirit of Louisiana into existence. "It just goes to show you," said Krissy, "you've got a good idea, and you get off your butt and do something about it, things like this happen." A domino effect of the noblest kind was triggered by a spur-of-the-moment outburst from one Louisiana man, a bit of prodding from his wife, and a swell of support from people who rallied to help him realize his goal.

In the end, the people of Louisiana raised $1.2 million, which went to purchase several more vehicles for the New York City Fire Department, including two special duty vehicles, the Heart of Louisiana, also known as "Spirit 2", and the Soul of Louisiana, or "Spirit 3". But the story doesn't end there.

Little did anyone know that, less than four years later, The Spirit of Louisiana would return to the state of its conception to help respond and rebuild after Hurricane Katrina devastated Louisiana's Gulf Coast in August of 2005. A total of 343 New York City firefighters, the same number lost in 9/11, also came down to provide assistance after Katrina.

Then, in 2012, the Spirit was dispatched back to New York to support recovery efforts after Hurricane Sandy, where it remained for several months before returning to Louisiana. The two cities, separated by 1200 miles, continue to enjoy a unique and lasting connection, thanks to one man's idea and, of course, his decision to "get off his butt and do something."

Brandon Fisher

Copiapó, Chile

The Chilean Mine Collapse

Do you remember watching the Chilean mine collapse incident unfold in Copiapó, Chile in 2010? If so, what images come to mind when you think of the rescue of those 33 trapped miners? Most of us remember that impossibly narrow, red-white-and-blue capsule sent down to rescue each of the men. But what do we recall of the challenges faced by the rescue workers or the lengths they went to in order to drill down and reach the miners in time?

When my friend Marty Plevel told me about Brandon Fisher, an American from Pennsylvania, and his involvement with the Chilean mine rescue, I knew I had to include his story in my book. At first, I didn't think I stood a chance of landing an interview with him. Why would he take time out of his busy schedule to talk with some unknown Canadian crisis consultant and author? I decided to take a shot and left Brandon a long, detailed voicemail message, not really expecting to hear back from him anytime soon. Later that week, however, he returned my call and agreed to share his experience with me. I was ecstatic!

A few weeks later, I made the journey to Berlin, Pennsylvania, and spent the day with Brandon, who recounted his captivating story and introduced me to some of the other men and women ultimately responsible for saving the lives of 33 Chilean miners.

Brandon's story poignantly illustrates that there are no borders when it comes to disasters. We're all in this together.

Dispatched from beneath 700,000 tons of rock, printed in red ink on a small slip of lined paper, the note read simply: Estamos bien en el refugio los 33. "We're doing well in the refuge, the 33." In Copiapó, Chile, a massive collapse in a metal mine had trapped thirty-three men, and rescuers had finally managed to discover their location. The world received the news that the miners, for whom hope had started to dwindle, were all alive and well with as much shock as joy. It was August 22, 2010, and this missive, wrapped around one of the rescuers' probes, was the first communication from the mine workers. So far, they'd spent seventeen days half a mile below the surface of the earth.

The Chilean miners had survived for so long because they'd had the good fortune to avoid some of the factors, like flooding, methane gas, and hypothermia, which have taken the lives of workers in other mine collapses. They rationed the small amount of food and water they had to share, and the larger-than-average safe room provided enough oxygen to support them all.

More than 4,500 miles away, in the small town of Berlin, Pennsylvania, Brandon Fisher and his wife, Julie, watched the coverage of the miners' first contact with the rescuers. Before this proof of life, the Fishers hadn't heard much about the Chilean mine collapse, but now it was big news, and they followed the story throughout the day, anxious to find out what the rescue plan would be. When Brandon heard that the engineers, in what would come to be called Plan A, would use raised-board drilling technology, he knew it would take months to reach the men. "That's a process where you drill a smaller hole down into the mine, then you put a larger bit on, and then pull from the surface back up," Brandon explains. Experts on the scene expected to free the miners sometime after Christmas, three months away. It didn't take Brandon long to realize he could help bring the men home much sooner.

Brandon holds patents but no degrees. As a high school student, he had his mind set on becoming a mechanical engineer, but he'd barely started on that journey, with just a few college credits under his belt and some experience working in the drilling industry, when he was offered a position running a project in Arkansas. Accepting the job would mean putting off school for two years, but Brandon decided the money and experience would be worth the delay in completing his education. "Well," says Brandon, "it isn't too often that you hear that turn into a success story because usually when someone postpones college to go into the working field, they earn the money and they never go back to college. Ultimately, that's what happened to me, but it launched my career."

The project, the Beaver Dam Cutoff in Eureka Springs, Arkansas, turned out to be one of the biggest drilling projects in United States history. It exposed the nineteen-year-old to hands-on experience and connected him with Ingersoll-Rand engineers, so that when the project wrapped he had a plethora of job offers. Thus, a career in the drilling industry was born. It's an industry in which there's a constant need for innovation—new ideas, new products—because every drilling situation is different. Brandon says, "Mother Nature didn't put the same thing in two places twice. Rocks are different. Ground conditions are different. It's always a challenge."

In 1998, Brandon Fisher founded Center Rock Inc., a drilling company that specializes in products and services that can handle uniquely challenging operating conditions, like drilling horizontal holes, through solid rock, under highways and rivers. In 2002, Center Rock participated in a rescue that saved the lives of nine miners in the "Miracle at Quecreek," a near disaster in which the men came close to drowning after incomplete information led them to break through the wall of an abandoned mine, releasing seventy-two million gallons of water. Brandon says the rescue happened in spite of the fact that they worked with inferior equipment, and neither the mining community nor the government was prepared for such emergencies.

Fast forward back to August 2010, and we find the drilling expert monitoring the news and contemplating what Center Rock could do for the thirty-three Chilean miners. Brandon Fisher called a meeting with Richard Soppe, a senior engineer and senior drilling technician, and Rudy Lyon, another engineer with the company. The men were in three different states at the time, so they conferenced by phone. Though they had no contacts in Chile or with anyone involved in the rescue efforts, they wanted to figure out if they could use their unique equipment and expertise to help. Brandon says, "No one had ever drilled a hole with a system like ours, to that depth, [over] that time period, and [through] that rock. We knew all the challenges were out there, but we felt we did have a legitimate chance to do this and do it quicker."

Once the trio convinced themselves the odds were good that they could make a difference, they faced the more challenging step of figuring out how to get in touch with the right people. They scoured the Internet for days to find a way to contact the mining engineers already involved in the rescue, but came up empty. Brandon and his men then reached out to Governor Ed Rendell of Pennsylvania, their home state. They succeeded in connecting with Rendell, who happened to be traveling with Secretary of State Hillary Clinton.

Unfortunately, the governor declined to get involved in the situation, and the United States government seemed to be sending a typical foreign policy message: "We will not get involved unless the Chilean government contacts our government and asks for help." The men of Center Rock would have to find a connection to Chile elsewhere.

As luck would have it, Brandon's wife had recently started a relationship between Center Rock and The Southern Allegheny Planning and Development Commission, a non-profit agency that promotes commerce between Pennsylvania manufacturing companies and other countries.

Center Rock's Brandon Fisher fabricating a fishing tool that was used to at-tempt to recover broken pieces of the 12" x 5.5" drill bit that broke when it hit a roof bolt at the depth of 262 meters. Photo credit: Richard Soppe

Chilean President Sebastián Piñera signing the side of the first 28" x 12" LP drill before it is lowered in the ground. Photo credit: Brandon Fisher

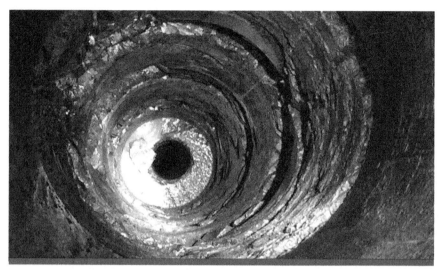

The view looking down the first 30′ of the rescue shaft. The dark circle in the center is the 12″ pilot hole that the 28″ tool was following.
Photo credit: Brandon Fisher

"33" bracelets – This picture was taken and sent to Brandon and the Center Rock team in Chile by a few CR employees as a show of support and to encourage them to keep pushing onward. Photo credit: Center Rock Inc.

Center Rock's Brandon Fisher and Richard Soppe with their Chilean counter-part Igor Proestakis, in front of the original mine entrance, just minutes before they left the site to return to the U.S. for the last time. Photo credit: Center Rock Inc.

Center Rock's Richard Soppe sending birthday wishes to his daughter halfway across the world, from Chile to America! Photo credit: Brandon Fisher

The organization had key contacts in Chile and was able to connect Brandon with the right people. Within a day, Sergio Sanchez, a contact in Santiago, Chile, had Brandon and his men on the phone with engineers from Codelco, the mining company in charge of the rescue.

Center Rock's experience with Quecreek and other rescues in the United States lent serious validity to the ideas Brandon proposed. Igor Proestakis, a young field engineer with Drillers Supply, one of Center Rock's distributors, was on the rescue site and quickly understood that Center Rock's technology was right for the job. He became the key contact for Brandon and his men, and after a week and a half of teleconferences, officials welcomed Center Rock's help. Together they came up with "Plan B."

In this new plan, Brandon would use a technology known as down-the-hole (DTH) drilling to follow one of the five-and-a-half-inch holes drilled by the rescuers on the scene, widening it to twelve inches. Then Center Rock's Low Profile Drill (L.P. Drill), which employed four or five hammers instead of just one, would widen the hole to twenty-eight inches to allow for passage of the rescue capsule. To contend with the large debris field that resulted from the collapse, they'd need to drill on an angle through hard rock to reach the men over 2,000 feet below. Brandon puts the idea of "hard rock" into perspective as he explains, "Berry granite, which is kind of known as the 'rock of ages' here in the United States for headstones, is about 22,000 psi in terms of hardness. The rock that we drilled in Chile was 39,000 psi, so it's much, much harder than some of the hardest granite we have here in the United States."

The equipment required to complete this mission wasn't the type of paraphernalia they could pull off the shelf. It had to be manufactured on demand, and Center Rock's employees worked around the clock to get things done as quickly as possible.

A cold morning picture from the "Plan B" site, looking at the "Plan C" rig. Photo credit: Brandon Fisher

Chilean head geologist Filipe Mathews with all 4 Center Rock LP Drills used to drill the rescue shaft. Photo credit: Brandon Fisher

The first of the 28" x 12" LP drills being installed on the drill rig. Photo credit: Brandon Fisher

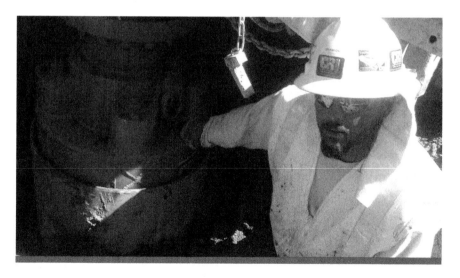

Brandon Fisher beside the first 28" LP drill just minutes before the team started drilling the 12" hole out to the rescue diameter. Photo credit: Richard Soppe

Brandon describes the "33 Lives" signs people posted around the office as reminders. "Everyone put motivational stuff up," he says, "because there was no point in sleeping." Outside vendors working on the equipment went into the same non-stop production mode. Center Rock manufactured the three hole openers needed for the first phase of the plan within thirty-six hours. The process normally takes two weeks.

The plan required two waves of equipment to be shipped to Chile. The first wave, which included everything needed to drill the pilot hole, weighed between 10,000 and 15,000 pounds. Estimates to transport this equipment to Copiapó came in around $250,000. Fortunately, one of Center Rock's employees reached a UPS agent who figured out the equipment was for the Chilean mine rescue and put Center Rock in touch with UPS's humanitarian relief program. "Long story short," says Brandon, "they flew all that equipment down to Chile for free, which was amazing."

At that point, Brandon and Richard turned their full attention to traveling to Chile, where they would build the equipment and drill the hole. They anticipated that the job would take thirty-five days, which meant Brandon's small company would be without its founder for over a month. Center Rock would have to run without them. "That was indeed a tough decision," says Brandon, "to take me out of the company, to take one of my senior guys out of the company, and go to a remote area of Chile for that long. The other issue that we had, by manufacturing this equipment, we really had to shut our facilities down and focus them one hundred percent on supporting this mine rescue effort. It's a scary thing for any business to tell your customers we can't help you right now." But those customers responded with understanding and offers of support, and on September 4, 2010, thirteen days after they first contemplated getting involved, Brandon Fisher and senior engineer Richard Soppe arrived in Copiapó, Chile.

Within two days, the pair had the equipment set up to start drilling. They were joined by representatives from the international drilling community, including Canadians, Chileans, and others from the United States. They would be onsite for thirty-seven days. "Out of that thirty-seven days," says Brandon, "we slept in beds seven times, Richard and I." For the first week, they grabbed the occasional nap in an empty truck. Then the Chilean Army came in and provided a tent for the men. Later they upgraded their sleeping quarters to a shipping container. "Once in a while, we'd have transitions, trip time coming in and out of the hole. We'd see like a ten-hour break, so we could run to town, which was like a forty-five-minute drive. We'd get a hotel room, get a real shower, sleep in a real bed." The minimal sleep and around-the-clock work, day after day, would leave both men with serious health issues that would require medical intervention and time to heal once the job was done.

Throughout the process, Brandon had frequent doubts about their chances for success. The hole turned out to be much more severely angled than they'd expected, and they had to do some redesigning on the fly. There were breakdowns, geological obstacles, and mechanical problems. "I don't know if there was a minute of every day that we were there that we weren't scared to death that something was going to keep us from being successful down there. It was a lot of praying, a lot of yelling, a lot of screaming. It was all in on every front," says Brandon.

In the end, it took thirty-three days to dig the hole through which the rescue capsule could reach the trapped miners. "The morning that we finished the hole it was such an overwhelming feeling, I'll never forget it for the rest of my life," says Brandon. Thousands of reporters and onlookers witnessed the achievement, and millions more watched it on television. But for Brandon and Richard, the sense of relief and accomplishment didn't last long. Within a couple of hours, the men went from a focus on finishing their drilling job to an urgent need to clear out, so the next phase of the rescue could get underway.

Brandon's wife, Julie, had spent the final two weeks of the drilling effort in Chile with Brandon and Richard, and the three flew back home together. As they headed to baggage claim at the Pittsburgh airport, they noticed a group of reporters in the area. Brandon assumed a professional athlete or some other celebrity must be arriving—until the reporters swarmed his small group. "We didn't have television when we were down there," he explains. "We could see thousands of reporters, and obviously we did interviews and stuff like that, but it didn't really hit us until we got home that the whole world really was watching this entire event." It was their first inkling of how big the story really was. They drove back to Berlin to find the town hung with signs welcoming them home. Brandon says it was both humbling and "an awesome feeling."

Three days later, the employees of Center Rock joined the Fishers at their home to gather around the television and watch as the miners, one by one, returned to their families through the hole Center Rock had dug. Brandon still chokes up when he talks about that moment. "This company did the rescue," he says. "Not just us, there were thousands of people involved in that rescue. But to see our employees sitting there, and realizing that they were a part of something that big and something that good—you could see the smiles on their faces and the tears in their eyes when all their hard work paid off and worked out."

As he sat surrounded by the small team that had joined him in making it possible for thirty-three men to return to their friends and families in half the expected time, Brandon Fisher had no idea that he'd soon have the opportunity to meet a couple of the miners at an event in Boston. To his surprise, they would recall a conversation they had with him while they were in the mine, referring to him in the emotional meeting, filled with handshakes, hugs, and tears, as "the guy with the bad Spanish."

Nor did Brandon have any inkling that a few months later he and his wife would sit in the guest box with First Lady Michelle Obama as President Obama gave the State of the Union Address. The small-town entrepreneur, who combines creativity and entrepreneurship to build a business that not only seeks to profit but also seeks to serve, would listen as Mr. Obama used the story of Brandon Fisher and Center Rock Inc. as a living example of the American Dream, an example of why we have a hopeful future, an example of ordinary people that do extraordinary things.

Rebecca and Genevieve Williams

Joplin, Missouri

The 2011 Joplin Tornado

When I first heard about Rebecca and Genevieve Williams through an industry colleague and friend, Jock Menzies, he referred to them as "sheroes," and the term stuck. To this day, I can't help but refer to this dynamic mother-daughter duo as "sheroes" whenever I share their story. These "social media in emergency management" trailblazers provided a new model for the way we communicate after disasters. Moved to action by the deadly 2011 tornado in Joplin, Missouri, they were the first to use social media, particularly Facebook, to share disaster information and resources with the public in an organized, well-coordinated manner.

I sat down with Rebecca and Genevieve in Joplin less than two years after the tornado, and I felt an instant connection with these #smem (social media in emergency management) pioneers. Rebecca and Genevieve have since gone on to create or oversee numerous other successful Facebook pages, including the Ebola Virus Info page. Their initiative demonstrates the importance of innovation, social connectivity, and openness to new technologies when responding to disasters. They also happen to be the most inspiring mother-daughter duo I know.

On May 22, 2011, the deadliest single tornado to hit an American city since the 1940s touched ground in Joplin, Missouri, instantly disrupting thousands of lives with a catastrophe of the kind that leaves a community, and a nation, stunned. Even before residents could begin to regroup, two women took it upon themselves to create a resource that would address the hopes, fears, and needs of those affected by the tragedy. Rebecca and Genevieve Williams, mother and daughter, are not only heroes; they're innovators who saw in a technology that most considered trivial and superficial an opportunity to solve problems in a new way.

The people of the state of Missouri know all too well the realities of living in an area prone to tornadoes. Since 1950, when the National Weather Service began tracking occurrences, the state has seen almost two thousand confirmed tornadoes, and on average, four of the state's residents lose their lives to these events each year. Despite the potential danger, residents carry on with their normal lives as watches and warnings are issued throughout tornado season.

Such was the case on that spring Sunday, a day that was to be one of the most memorable thus far in the young lives of the seniors of Joplin High School. That afternoon, the teenagers, bubbling with the mix of excitement and trepidation that graduation brings, concluded their time as high school students with a ceremony held at Missouri Southern State University. Neither the students nor their families could've imagined that a day filled with joy, and pride, and anticipation of the opportunities and experiences that lay ahead of the graduates would end with their former school building ripped apart, or that the university athletic center where they received their diplomas would soon be converted into a Red Cross evacuation center for scores of displaced homeowners.

Left to right: Genevieve Williams, David Burton from the University of Missouri, and Rebecca Williams. Photo credit: Suzanne Bernier

The butterfly mural is on 15th and Main in Joplin, and was completed in Nov 2011. It depicts 'The Butterfly People' the children in the tornado zone thought they saw that day. Photo credit: Michelle Short

Even though St. Mary's Church isn't a memorial, it was one of the most recognized places in Joplin. Photo credit: Michelle Short

The Victims' memorial in Cunningham Park became a time capsule on the 1st anniversary of the 2011 Joplin tornado. Photo credit: Michelle Short

In the minutes before the tornado struck, Rebecca Williams and her twenty-three-year-old daughter, Genevieve, gathered with their family for Sunday dinner at the home of Rebecca's parents, just fifteen miles south of Joplin, under a dark and foreboding sky. As they came to the table, the outdoor warning sirens in nearby Newton County sounded a call for people to take shelter, but as Genevieve points out, that wouldn't be enough to send most locals running for cover. At that time of year, the sirens blared so often few people would drop what they were doing every time they heard the warning. As for Genevieve, Rebecca, and their family, they carried on with dinner.

It wasn't that they doubted the existence of the threat. They'd seen several tornadoes over the years, but the seemingly random nature of the events, and the inability to predict where the funnel might touch down, created a sense that as long as the tornado hadn't been sighted, there wasn't much to be done. Still, the family didn't take their safety for granted. While they dined, they listened to the weather radio and kept an eye on the television news. Live images of the tornado brought an end to the meal.

As Joplin residents picked up last minute party supplies to celebrate the graduation, gassed up cars after church, or whiled away the Sunday afternoon, the tornado barreled toward their city. Rebecca says the seriousness of the moment hit home for her family when they witnessed something rarely seen on television. The normally unflappable news anchors abandoned the news desk to take cover. "So there was a little bit of warning," Rebecca says, "but by the time they did that, the tornado had already started hitting part of Joplin."

To make matters worse, a torrential downpour obscured the movements of the tornado. "It was rain-wrapped," explains Rebecca. "You'd go to the door, and you'd look, and you wouldn't have seen anything. It totally changed my perspective on everything storm-related." The conditions prevented many people, including some of those who'd attended the Joplin High School graduation ceremony, from putting enough distance between themselves and the tornado.

A mother and her teenage daughter, on their way to pick up a cake for the daughter's graduation party, were trapped in their car as the tornado piled vehicle on top of vehicle. A young man and his father raced to outrun the tornado, but their sport-utility vehicle overturned, a seat belt snapped, and the terrible winds snatched the young man through the sunroof. His body would be found in a nearby pond. Two teenagers sought shelter in a grocery store parking lot; one awakened in the hospital, only to discover the tornado had taken his friend. While most of the students of Joplin High School survived, two were counted among the 161 people who perished in the indiscriminate violence of the event.

At its largest, the funnel grew to almost a mile wide, and in the course of the thirty-eight minutes it spent on the ground, it cut a seven-mile swath through Joplin, demolishing everything in its path. Rebecca, Genevieve, and their relatives had the tremendous good fortune to be outside of the tornado's strike zone, and while the winds and hurricane-force rains damaged their homes, the structures remained standing. With electrical power and landlines both knocked out, they couldn't flip on the news or call friends to inquire about what damage had been done throughout the area. However, they still had their charged iPhones, and even without cellular phone service, they could access the Internet.

Through one of the two thousand followers of a Facebook page she'd maintained since high school, Genevieve received word that a Joplin hospital, St. John's Regional Medical Center, had sustained massive damage. The 341-bed institution later released security footage that shows a stark scene as the vacant emergency room becomes a chaotic swirl of furniture, fixtures, and wiring tossed and churned by powerful winds as the tornado roars through the building.

Though hospital personnel worked to secure the safety of everyone onsite, one visitor and five patients lost their lives.

However, in the immediate aftermath of the storm, no one could confirm whether or not there'd been casualties. Thus, within two hours of the tornado strike, Rebecca and Genevieve simply reported, "St. John's has been hit. That's all we know for sure," and with those words, launched the Joplin Tornado Info Facebook page. In the following weeks, the mother-daughter team would update and moderate the page around the clock, as the community labored to recover from the scores of lost lives, hundreds of injuries, more than seven thousand destroyed homes, and hundreds of impacted businesses.

In the beginning, Joplin Tornado Info advised readers as to where they could find triage areas, fresh water and food, and other resources to meet immediate needs. They posted a request that people with functioning laptops gather at Missouri Southern State University. There, the laptop owners cooperated to provide a means for anyone who could travel to the university to email friends and relatives or register on safeandwell.org, a Red Cross site designed to allow people to search for the names of their loved ones among a database of survivors. In another sign of the times, charging stations were set up at a local university so residents could charge their devices, making it easier to continually monitor Joplin Tornado Info and other news sources.

To those looking in from the outside, the use of social media at a time like this might have seemed frivolous, but while most cellular service and landlines remained down for weeks, many cell phones could still send and receive text messages or access the Internet. Rebecca posted a call for Facebook users in the area to "Please like this page, so it may grow and be of use," and people responded. The page quickly grew to be recognized as one of the most accurate, consistent, and accessible ways to stay abreast of tornado-related news.

A mobile first aid and supply depot was set up just hours after the tornado in the Joplin High School parking lot on 20th street - in the background is the ruins of the Franklin Tech building. Photo credit: Michelle Short

The corner of 26th and Maiden Lane, where a Pronto gas station and pharmacy used to reside - someone placed two teddy bears among the steel beams for two lost children in the tornado. Photo credit: Michelle Short

Joplin High School becomes "Hope" High following the 2011 tornado. Photo credit: Michelle Short

Such reliance from the population of Joplin proved a heavy responsibility, and as they realized the magnitude of what they'd taken on, Genevieve and Rebecca began to build a team. They recruited co-administrators to monitor what news sources and individuals reported about rescue and recovery efforts and to moderate what followers wrote on the page. As the page grew, administrators made a point of responding to everyone who left a comment, a simple act that built trust between them and the community. Recognizing from the outset the importance of protecting the integrity of Joplin Tornado Info, they also made the decision to ban a short list of people who failed to respect the guidelines they'd set forth.

With the group they assembled, there was always someone with the right connections or resources to find answers and corroborate or disprove new information. Some rumors that had been posted and shared on Facebook enough to go viral—tales of children abandoned in a local hospital and crying for their parents, stories of the systematic euthanizing of pets at the animal shelter—proved untrue, and the administrators quickly discredited the falsehoods, setting minds at ease.

In other cases, Joplin Tornado Info became a resource of last resort, a haven for hopes with no other outlet. In one such instance, a woman called to request a post be added to the page. Her brother's vehicle had been spotted at a home improvement store, but there was no sign of him, and she was hoping someone who knew of his whereabouts would see the post and respond. "We looked at each other and shook our heads," says Rebecca. "We knew that person was not among the living. It turned out they were not. It was weird because we just knew, and I'm sure the woman knew, too…"

The Spirit Tree is one of many trees destroyed by a deadly tornado that struck Joplin on May 22, 2011. Months later, local artists painted it in bright shades, symbolizing the new spirit of the community. Each color represents different things - white is spirit, red is life, yellow is knowledge, black is clarity, blue is prayer, purple is healing, and orange is kinship with other living creatures. The tree is a tribute to the 161 people who lost their lives, and to honour both the survivors and many volunteers who came to help Joplin recover. The "Spirit Tree" is a symbol of the unity and resilience of the residents of Joplin. Photo credit: Michelle Short

In addition to the weight of those pleas for assistance to which they could provide no satisfactory response, Rebecca and Genevieve dealt with significant push-back from some of the established disaster rescue and relief organizations. At the time, most of them only used social media in a limited way, if at all. They certainly didn't rely on those websites to share real-time updates on an ongoing crisis, and they took issue with what they saw as inexperienced civilians jumping in to do a job best left to the experts. Representatives contacted the women and strongly suggested they take down the page.

Confident in their ability to make a worthwhile contribution, mother and daughter persisted. Few of their critics were aware that, between the two of them, they had experience in social media strategy, journalism, public relations, copy writing, broadcasting, logistics, and psychiatric nursing. These skill sets, and the diverse and deep knowledge of other volunteers, lifted the site above what could be considered an amateur effort. Still, as does any fledgling endeavor, Joplin Tornado Info suffered a few missteps. Genevieve remembers one such instance with a keen sense of sorrow and regret.

In the pre-dawn hours of the morning following the storm, Genevieve monitored the police radio through an application on her smartphone. Struggling with exhaustion after a long night with no sleep, she nevertheless wanted to relay any relevant information she heard. Rather than breaking to rest, she remained hyper-vigilant, determined to communicate anything that might assist or inform the citizens of Joplin. When local police called for twenty body bags to be delivered to a residential area populated with apartment complexes, she reported the news on Facebook, and within minutes, found herself reeling from the vitriolic responses popping up on Joplin Tornado Info. Readers condemned her, cursed her, and made death threats against her. Reflecting back on her decision to post what seemed in the moment an important fact from a solid source, Genevieve says, "I should never have done it."

Rebecca understands the emotional turmoil at the root of such extreme reactions. "Think of it this way," she says. "If your loved one lived in an apartment complex at 20th and Connecticut, and you were in Canada following social media, would you want to read on Facebook that twenty body bags had been called for in that area?" Even though she empathizes with the backlash from readers, the former psychiatric nurse has a pragmatic perspective on her daughter's controversial action. "I think she made the right call," says Rebecca, "because I've since learned that Red Cross, FEMA, the chainsaw people from the Baptist church—all the organizations look to social media in the early times to assess how bad things are to see whether or not they need to deploy." Given that the sun set just two hours after the tornado hit, no one had surveyed the full extent of the damage, and publicizing such a graphic, shocking detail sent a clear message: the tornado had devastated Joplin.

This was taken approximately 15 minutes before the tornado, and was taken from resident Michelle Short's front yard on Moffet Avenue as the storm rolled in. She never imagined those clouds would change so many lives forever. Photo credit: Michelle Short

Shocked and hurt by the response from the very people she'd set out to serve, Genevieve questioned whether she should leave the disaster communications to the professionals. After finally getting a few hours' sleep and talking things over with her mother, she realized that she should continue, but to do so required putting aside her ego and developing a thick skin. That decision to make a concerted effort to resist taking things personally would serve her well as the Joplin Tornado Info team continued its work.

Genevieve and Rebecca remained committed to their mission, and the list of services their one Facebook page provided in the coming weeks and months is a long one. Out-of-towners kept up with the page and text messaged updates to locals who couldn't access the Internet. Many followers left comments in an attempt to locate missing loved ones, and to make their search a little easier, a volunteer created a directory of all the local hospitals to which previous St. John's patients and tornado victims had been taken. Loads of donated goods arrived well before official organizations were set up to manage their distribution, and when the truckers called the phone number on Joplin Tornado Info, Genevieve and Rebecca made sure they found a place to drop off the goods, so no donations would be turned away. When the page's administrators posted about the need for Port-a-Potties to accommodate the many relief effort volunteers, a reader in Massachusetts reached out to help, and this basic necessity made its way to Joplin. When a load of donated mattresses needed to be delivered, Genevieve coordinated a relay of truckers to haul the cargo from Omaha, Nebraska. This online community established by a mother and daughter, with little more than a couple of smart phones and the desire to be a part of the solution, brought together individuals, organizations, and businesses across the nation in support of Joplin.

Along with their co-administrators, the two women continue to run Joplin Tornado Info, sharing information about severe weather events and other local emergencies and providing education on disaster preparedness. Out of their experience, they produced a guidebook, The Use of Social Media for Disaster Recovery, which outlines best practices for anyone thinking of launching and running a similar site. In conjunction with University of Missouri Extension, they published the book as a downloadable document available to the public at no charge, and people and groups in several other cities and towns have used their example to establish their own social media presence for disaster communications. Many of the organizations that initially tried to dissuade Rebecca and Genevieve from continuing with the Facebook page now distribute the booklet, and the Federal Emergency Management Agency has used it in trainings nationwide.

In 2012, one year after the tornado ripped through the city, President Barack Obama traveled to Joplin to give the commencement address at Joplin High School's graduation ceremony. Speaking to students and their families, many of whom had lost homes, friends, relatives, businesses, or jobs, he expanded on a quote from Joplin City Manager, Mark Rohr, who'd declared that Joplin residents chose to be defined by their response, not by the tragedy. President Obama said, "We can define our lives not by what happens to us, but by how we respond. We can choose to carry on. We can choose to make a difference in the world."

Rebecca Williams and her daughter, Genevieve Williams, chose to respond in an innovative manner that served the community in a time of profound grief and need. They chose to employ all their knowledge, experience, and resources in helping the people of Joplin recover, rebuild, and carry on. They chose to serve one city and, in doing so, created a new strategy that has touched and benefited communities near and far, and their work continues to make a difference in the world to this day.

Mohamed Gouda

New York, New York

U.S. Airways Flight 1549, "Miracle on the Hudson"

One day in 2013, while I was on a ferry tour of the Hudson River, our guide mentioned that our captain was one of the first to rescue some of the passengers from U.S. Airways Flight 1549, often referred to as "The Miracle on the Hudson." I perked up as soon as I heard that, and I made sure to introduce myself to Captain Mohamed Gouda at the end of the tour. Following a brief but extremely interesting chat, Captain Gouda agreed to meet with me the following month to share his memories of the event.

I imagine most Americans recall watching footage of Flight 1549's remarkable landing on the Hudson River. Many news followers likely also remember the name of the hero in that dramatic landing, Captain Chesley Sullenberger, or "Captain Sully." The pilot pulled off a remarkable feat, and the accolades he received were richly deserved. However, there were many other heroes that day, each of whom worked to ensure all the stranded passengers and crew made it safely to shore. One of those heroes is Captain Mohamed Gouda. This is his story.

Captain Mohamed Gouda with retired U.S. Airlines Captain Chesley Burnett "Sully" Sullenberger, III at a ceremony recognizing their heroic actions following the "Miracle on the Hudson" on January 15, 2009. Photo credit: unknown (personal photo provided by Captain Mohamed Gouda)

Not yet fluent in English and without a concrete plan of what he could do to earn a living, twenty-year-old Mohamed Gouda immigrated to the United States from Egypt in 1998 with high expectations. "I came full of dreams of opportunities, and brilliant ideas, and a great future," he says. But instead of instant career success, Mohamed found himself taking whatever employment he could find in stores, warehouses, and factories—not exactly what he'd moved almost 6,000 miles from the place of his birth to do. He'd greatly underestimated the difficulties inherent in building a life from scratch in a foreign land. Young Mohamed needed full-time work, something that could sustain him and allow him to live independently.

In those early weeks, Mohamed used his free time to look for work and to explore what many consider the most vibrant and diverse city of his new country. He took the train from New Jersey, where he stayed with relatives, to New York City, where he visited the World Trade Center and gravitated to South Street Seaport. As he watched the boats come and go, the commuter ferries caught his attention, and he decided to take a chance and see if he could get work on one of them. When he approached ferry workers and inquired as to how he could get a similar job, Mohamed was focused on stable employment and financial security. He would find much more. He would find his calling.

With no previous experience, he convinced the company management that he was more capable than his limited command of English might imply, and after repeated calls to ask if they were hiring yet, he landed an entry-level position fueling watercraft. But the workings of the boats piqued Mohamed's curiosity. He constantly asked questions, absorbing everything he could about this new environment. When he learned the company planned to lay off fuelers, Mohamed asked to be promoted to deckhand. He continued to expand his knowledge and eventually learned to drive the boat. He served as a deckhand for six years before his former captain, promoted to manager and later to vice president, encouraged him to reach higher. In 2005, Mohamed passed the difficult licensing test with a score of 100% on each section and received another promotion. Mohamed Gouda, one-time boat-fueler, was now Captain Gouda.

Back and forth, back and forth, back and forth across the waters of the Hudson River, commuters and tourists on the ferry between New Jersey and New York likely give little thought to what's involved in making the eight-minute journey happen safely and efficiently each day. For most passengers, it's a chance to read the newspaper or steal a quiet moment before work. Few think about the responsibility the captain bears as he takes on up to four hundred passengers. Normally, things go smoothly, and it's easy to take for granted that they always will.

With more than a decade at work on those waters, Captain Gouda knows better than most that a day on the river isn't always so uneventful. While his first obligation is to his passengers, crew, and boat—an obligation that requires ever more vigilance in these times of heightened awareness of terrorist threats—Captain Gouda feels the same sense of responsibility for anyone who shares the waterway.

That sense of duty to others came into play on an otherwise ordinary day when the crew of the Katherine G ran into trouble. From half a mile away, aboard the ferry he shuttled between New York and New Jersey, Captain Gouda watched the tugboat maneuver a crane. The tug was just off Liberty Island, the small piece of land from which the Statue of Liberty gazes out at New York Harbor. As the captain observed from a distance, the tug started to tilt. It fell over on its side and sunk in a matter of seconds, taking the sixty-ton crane, brought to the island for use in restoration of the statue, with it. It was just before ten in the morning on Good Friday, April 6, 2012, and Captain Gouda's was the only boat in the area.

He contacted Vessel Traffic Service and requested help. But there were men overboard and no time to wait for responders to arrive. Grateful that he wasn't carrying any passengers, Captain Gouda drove to the scene of the Katherine G's accident. "As soon as I arrived there," he says, "I saw three people swimming on the water. I saw three people fighting for their lives." Captain Gouda needed to get closer, but if he hit the sunken tugboat or the submerged crane, he could capsize his own boat, making the predicament much worse for everyone involved.

With the current moving quickly and water temperatures low enough to cause hypothermia in a matter of minutes, the captain maneuvered the boat as Marquis Mainor, the deckhand, lowered the rescue ladder and threw out a lifeline to pull in the men and bring them aboard the Father Mychal Judge, the New York Waterway ferry named for the first fireman to die in the September 11th terrorist attack on the World Trade Center.

As he boarded the ferry, the captain of the sunken ship shook with cold and with the shock of his loss. "He had just seen his boat disappear in front of his eyes. I don't blame the guy," says the soft-spoken Captain Gouda. "As a captain, when your own house goes down, it's sad." The other two men, a park police officer and a Coast Guard officer, followed.

Still in an area that placed his boat at great risk because of rocks and debris, Captain Gouda confirmed with his new passengers that there were no others needing rescue and made a hasty return to deeper waters. While the Katherine G would have to be scrapped, none of the men suffered serious injuries.

The whole thing happened quickly, and Captain Gouda had little time to plan out his response. He saw a crew in need of help and acted to save them. "It's my job," he says. "If you see somebody in danger, you just have to react and take action." The quick decision to provide aid may have come instinctively for him because it wasn't the first time he'd played a part in a rescue on the water.

Three years before the tugboat incident, on January 15, 2009, Captain Gouda started his 3:00 p.m. shift with his usual check of his boat. As he and his crew left the dock, the captain noticed, just above the sun, a plane flying low over the George Washington Bridge. "It was kind of amazing," he says. "It took my attention, and I kept looking at it. It was something very, very hard to believe, and every second I kept saying, that plane is going back up. It's going back up."

But US Airways Flight 1549, piloted by Captain Chesley "Sully" Sullenberger III and First Officer Jeff Skiles, did not pull up. Just after take-off from LaGuardia, the plane had lost both engines in a bird strike, and they couldn't make it to the nearest airport. Instead, Captain Sullenberger made the decision to crash land in the river. As the Airbus touched down on the Hudson, it looked like it might be submerged, but it rose back above the water and slowed to a stop.

Captain Gouda held his breath, expecting a fire or explosion of the sort one might see in a movie version of a plane crash, but instead of a flame-licked, smoke-laden, chaotic scene, he witnessed relative calm and order as emergency doors opened and passengers exited the cabin and climbed onto the wings of the plane. "I was scared something bad could happen, because I have people, I have a crew, I have a boat, and I'm responsible for my boat and my crew," he says. Even with these concerns in the back of his mind, it never occurred to Captain Gouda to do anything but assist the people in need of aid. The ferry captain alerted his deckhands and headed for the site of the crash.

As they approached the plane, Captain Gouda and his crew realized some of the passengers had already jumped into the freezing water, and they warned the others not to follow suit because they'd never make it to land. Several boats converged near the plane and the crews worked together to scoop people out of the river. They helped passengers climb or jump from the ice-coated wings of the plane to the decks of the boats. While they worked, the plane steadily took on water, and each boat moved as close to the drifting Airbus as it could get without running into it and causing it to sink faster. If that happened, the boat and the plane might go down together. "So we had to use the skills to maneuver the boat just perfectly to the wing," Captain Gouda explains.

As the rescue continued, Captain Gouda and his crew circled the plane to monitor how quickly it was sinking. As they went, the captain saw a woman slip from a wing of the plane. A swift current carried her away, and unable to keep herself afloat, she struggled and went under before popping up again. Acting quickly, Captain Gouda maneuvered his boat closer to the woman he would later learn didn't know how to swim. A rescue diver dropped from a helicopter and held on to her long enough for Captain Gouda and his crew to draw nearer and lift the woman from the water.

"When she got into my boat, she was completely frozen. She couldn't move her fingers. She couldn't move her legs, and she was just screaming." Captain Gouda says the woman repeated the same thing over and over. "Please don't let me die," she pleaded. He did his best to calm her and to assure her she had escaped any danger as they docked at Pier 79 and handed her over to emergency medical services.

The captain gives much of the credit for the rescue to his three deckhands on the George Washington that day. Pepe Carumba, Greg Pages, and Jose Torres all labored with their captain to bring nineteen people to the safety of their boat. He also lauds Captain Vincent Lombardi, whose boat arrived first to the scene and rescued fifty-six people. Captain Gouda explains that it took a team effort from several boats to bring all 155 people from the downed Airbus to safety. Captain Sullenberger, after walking the cabin of the plane to make sure everyone had evacuated, was the last to leave.

While many lives were saved that day, the woman they pulled from the freezing water had the greatest impact on Captain Gouda. Years later, he still hears her voice imploring him not to let her die.

The realization of how close she'd come to losing her fight against the cold grip of the river, of how close she'd come to becoming the single casualty of Flight 1549, deepened his appreciation for life. "I learned God is good," says the captain. "God loves us. He gives us another chance to live." When he later met the rescued woman and her family at a "Miracle on the Hudson" reunion, he shared the message with her, telling her, "Ma'am, God gave you another life, another chance to live, so you'd better not waste it. Love your children. Love your husband."

That all the passengers and crew safely made it from the plane held special significance for Captain Gouda since his experience with low-flying planes eight years earlier involved a national tragedy resulting in close to 3,000 deaths. As a deckhand, he'd stood on a boat and watched a plane come in from the north and crash into the World Trade Center's North Tower on September 11, 2001. Like most who saw it, he thought he'd just borne witness to a horrible accident—until a second plane came from the south, flying even lower. It circled the Statue of Liberty and then crashed into the South Tower. Captain Gouda describes a sense of disbelief as he and the rest of the crew watched that terrifying incident unfold. "We saw people jumping and flying from the windows. I saw the fire happen. When the two buildings fell and the people were running, we could see the dust right behind them," he recounts. "They would actually come to the waterline and jump in the water."

Unlike most people who watched the events of 9/11 with a sense of futility, the watercraft on the Hudson quickly engaged in aiding the survivors. Private boats, party boats, diving boats, ferries, tugs, the Coast Guard and police boats—any vessel that could traverse the river lent a hand with the evacuation, even though they had no idea if another attack might be imminent. "We moved thousands of people," says Captain Gouda.

In actuality, with bridges, tunnels, and highways closed, it's estimated that more than 500,000 people were transported by water as they fled the dust, the debris, and the unknown. In an eight-hour span, the watercraft executed the largest boatlift in history. The vessels carried people away from lower Manhattan and transported injured survivors to New Jersey as New York hospitals quickly exceeded capacity. In the days after the event, the ferries would bring firefighters from New Jersey over to New York to aid the New York Fire Department in its ongoing efforts. Captain Gouda points out that he was just a crew member at the time, just one of many who made the boatlift happen, but for him it was also the beginning of a career in which a willingness to aid those in need plays a central role.

As you might expect, for his service to others, often at risk to his personal safety, Captain Mohamed Gouda has received considerable accolades: an Outstanding Achievement medal presented by the Secretary of Transportation; a medal from the Marine History Society; meetings with politicians on the state and national levels, including Secretary of State Hilary Clinton; honors from the Seafarers International Union and Captain Gouda's employer, New York Waterway; letters, emails, and invitations from survivors.

He doesn't take such attention for granted. But Captain Gouda says there are other things that mean even more to him. It touches him when, away from his boat, people recognize him as the ferry captain. "Just to see the appreciation in normal people's eyes. They know what you're doing, and they know being a captain is not an easy job." That sort of respect makes him feel honored to practice his vocation. Still, the thing that makes him most proud is the recognition he gets closer to home. The husband and father of three explains that his kids love to tell their teachers and classmates how their father has saved people. "It makes me feel good to see the appreciation. It makes me feel good that I'm doing something good in life, that I'm being positive," Captain Gouda says, but his children say, "My daddy works on a ferry, and he's a hero."

Evan and Jeff Parness

New York, New York

2003 San Diego Wildfires

The Birth of "New York Says Thank You"

If you're from the New York City area, you've probably already heard of "New York Says Thank You" and its work with disaster survivors. You may even have seen the 2011 documentary film of the same name. But it's a big world, and outside the city most people are unaware of NYSTY's unusual origin. Charitable organizations are often born of tragedy, just as this one was, created as a result of the September 11th terrorist attacks. Still, there is something unique about this particular story.

Long before the "New York Says Thank You" Foundation became an organized entity, five-year-old Evan Parness had an idea that would enlist countless others to help rebuild communities following disasters. The dramatic undertaking sparked by the words of a small child reminds us that heroes come in all ages and sizes. While his father, Jeff, took action to make the boy's desire to help a reality, at its heart, this is Evan's story.

The Parness family on the initial cross-country truck drive from New York to San Diego in November 2003. Photo credit: Hillel Parness/New York Says Thank You Foundation

New York Says Thank You volunteers help to rebuild Baker Chapel U.M.C. in DeGonia Springs, Indiana on the 9/11 Anniversary, 2006. Photo credit: Sandra Hauser/ New York Says Thank You Foundation

It was November 1, 2003, and Jeff Parness had just yelled at his young sons. As siblings often do, Evan, five, and Josh, three, were arguing over a toy. Until that moment, Jeff had been under the impression that his boys never argued, but it wasn't the squabble between brothers that set him off. Jeff had tried to reason with Evan, to get him to see no single toy was worth fighting over. After all, the two boys had hundreds of toys between them, while children just a few blocks away from their large, newly renovated Manhattan apartment were lucky if they had a single toy to call their own.

But it was the day after Halloween, and the boys were still coming down from the energy and excitement of the party they'd enjoyed with the children in their building the night before. Reason and gratitude were the last things on their minds. They wanted what they wanted. The mixed emotions Jeff felt about moving to their large apartment and providing a life for his children that most would consider luxurious—a sort of achiever's guilt—only heightened his need to make his sons understand how fortunate they were. Frustrated with his inability to get through to the boys, Jeff gave himself a time out. He went to another room and flipped on a television news program.

Jeff landed on coverage of the damage done by three major wildfires that had burned through almost 400,000 acres of San Diego County just days earlier. One of the fires was, by itself, the largest in California history, and between the three, sixteen lives were lost and more than 3,000 structures were destroyed. As a reporter interviewed a woman whose family spent Halloween in an evacuation center, Jeff couldn't help drawing comparisons to his own family life. He and his wife and sons had enjoyed the camaraderie of their neighbors in the comfort and security of their apartment building. The mother on the news explained that the children living in the center also had a party to mark the day that for most kids equaled an abundance of sweet treats and safe frights and dressing up in costumes they've looked forward to wearing for weeks. Unfortunately, her daughter's treasured Sleeping Beauty costume had been left behind and lost in the fire.

Jeff called his older son, Evan, into the room to witness the little girl who'd lost everything she owned. The boys had visited relatives in San Diego, so Jeff was careful to explain that everyone they knew and loved was okay, but he wanted to convey how fortunate their family was to have more than enough material possessions, while imparting a lesson about the responsibilities that came with a life of relative privilege. He explained to Evan that the little girl had lost her home, and while Evan had worn three costumes the night before, the little girl had none. "I looked at him," says Jeff, "and I asked him what he would do to help a girl in that situation."

The five-year-old considered the question with due seriousness, and in the spirit of empathy and generosity Jeff had hoped to see earlier that day, Evan offered to send some of the toys he and his brother didn't use very often to the little girl. After mulling over the situation for another moment, he added that it might be a good idea to include some clothes and some coins. "He was thinking on his own," recalls Jeff, "of what else the little girl might've needed."

This was Jeff's first deliberate attempt to talk with Evan about community service or charitable giving. The boy's earnest response may have been inspired by the rabbi who visited his kindergarten class to teach the students about Mitzvah Day. Mitzvah is the Hebrew word for a good deed, and the rabbi had impressed upon the class the importance of doing good deeds for people in need. Whatever the reason, whatever the influence, something clicked, and Evan began to comprehend that he was in a position to provide for someone whose circumstances were not as stable as his own.

While Jeff was pleased to see his son demonstrating compassion, he also believed a father should teach his children to dream big. "Wait a second," he told Evan. "What if you collect toys from all the kids who live in the apartment building?"

Evan lit up at the idea, but Jeff was calculating all the work involved in such an undertaking. Collecting one box from each of the thirty-five floors, getting the boxes to a delivery service, and paying for cross-country shipping could prove to be time-consuming and expensive. It occurred to him that it might actually be more cost-effective to rent a truck and drive the donation to San Diego himself. The idea thrilled him.

In recent months, Jeff had been contemplating what his role as a father meant beyond the day-to-day duties and joys. The wisdom he could impart to his children, the legacy of character he could leave them—those were the things he wanted to be sure not to overlook. What a statement, he thought, he could make as a dad, if he showed Evan and Josh their family could do something tangible that made a significant difference in someone's life. Jeff couldn't help thinking a series of recent experiences—books he'd been reading on leadership and fatherhood, discussions about life's purpose, and reflections on his own upbringing—had led him to this moment.

He recalled a recent interview in which Rudy Giuliani, who was finishing his term as mayor of New York when the 9/11 terrorist attacks occurred, expressed his concern that just two years later, people were already forgetting the meaning of the infamous day. Jeff didn't want to forget what that event really meant. He couldn't forget. On the morning of September 11, 2001, Jeff's friend and business partner, Hagay Shefi, went to "Windows on the World" in the North Tower of the World Trade Center to speak at a risk management conference. Until they saw his aunt holding up his picture on television, Hagay's coworkers had no idea he'd been in the tower when the plane hit. His remains were among the first to be identified. Jeff says the thirty-four-year-old, who left behind a wife, two children, and his parents and two siblings, started every business meeting with a simple admonition: "Life is too short. Focus on what you love. Focus, focus, focus."

In the ensuing two years, Jeff struggled to find a way to honor his friend's memory and the philosophy he encouraged everyone around him to live by. Nothing seemed sufficient to commemorate Hagay's life, but making life a little easier for the people displaced by the wildfires might be a good start. Jeff thought, "We're going to drive a truck cross-country from New York to San Diego, filled with relief supplies, and I'm going to put a big sign on it that says, 'New York Says Thank You.'"

New York had plenty to be thankful for. In the aftermath of 9/11, people from big cities, expansive suburbs, and small towns most New Yorkers had never heard of sent money, supplies, and contingents of relief workers to the city. Jeff wanted his children to know and remember that on 9/12, more people than could be counted took action to make it clear that they stood with the people of New York City. The 2,800-mile truck drive would be his expression of gratitude on behalf of his fellow New Yorkers.

He recalls the excitement of that moment of vision. "You know when you think of big ideas and your heart starts racing out of your chest? That was me [then]. It hasn't stopped." After conferring with a friend who encouraged him to run with the plan, Jeff decided to wait and see how things looked in the morning. "You sleep on these big ideas sometimes," says Jeff, "and you're all psychologically torqued up, and the next morning you're not as connected to it. But I woke up the next morning, and I couldn't stop thinking about it."

He received his first contribution to the nascent "New York Says Thank You" that same day when he ran into a local restaurateur, with whom he was friendly, and shared his idea. The man, an immigrant from the Dominican Republic, felt so moved by Jeff's proposed mission and so appreciative of the opportunities his adopted country had afforded him, he donated $1,000 to kick off the effort. Once a couple of Jeff's friends committed to making the drive with him, there was no turning back.

They parked the truck, emblazoned with "New York Says Thank You," in front of the apartment building where the Parness family lived. People walking down the street stopped to ask what they were doing, and when they heard the story, many ducked into nearby stores and returned with bags brimming with donations. Many of the New Yorkers also shared their own 9/11 stories with Jeff and thanked him for acting on their behalf. "I'm sitting here watching this dynamic I never could've imagined," recalls Jeff, "thinking, oh, wait a second. This isn't just about the people in California. This is about giving people in New York the opportunity to resolve these intertwined emotions they still have about 9/11."

As they drove from the east coast to the west, Americans they met along the way made additional contributions, filling the truck. Because of a spontaneous conversation between a father and son, because that father was willing to take seriously, implement, and expand on the ideas of a five-year-old boy, hundreds of people became a part of a connection between survivors of 9/11 and survivors of the San Diego wildfires. The truck arrived in Southern California just nine days after Evan suggested he could sacrifice a few toys for children who no longer had any, and "New York Says Thank You" provided everything needed to outfit a recreation center for 300 children displaced by the wildfires.

In 2004, Jeff realized the idea of "New York Says Thank You" had to be bigger than one road trip, and hopping in the truck whenever disaster struck wasn't a sustainable plan. With a small group of friends, he incorporated the organization and looked for ways they could broaden their reach. At the time, the first 9/11 impact reports were being released, and they revealed that large numbers of first responders suffered from depression and other ongoing psychological harm. Jeff says, "We realized that at the core of this is the whole 9/11 experience, but also at the core of this was the 9/12 experience, what people were like the day after. Poetic justice would be to go build stuff for 9/11. It's the day you think about destruction and what came down. Let's put stuff up." His instincts told him there would be something inherently cathartic about making something positive out of such a devastating tragedy, and firefighters from the New York City Fire Department needed and deserved a chance to be involved.

Jeff had no connection to the fire department, but in a happy turn of fortune, the day after they incorporated the "New York Says Thank You" Foundation, he found a FDNY battalion command truck parked across from his home. Jeff couldn't pass up the opportunity to explain to one of the firefighters what he had in mind. It was the beginning of an ongoing relationship with the department, and that year, eleven New York City firefighters joined Jeff and a small crew and flew to San Diego to help rebuild houses destroyed by the wildfires. "Firefighters from all over Southern California showed up," says Jeff. "The whole town showed up. It was the most American thing I'd ever experienced."

It was also an experience that would shape the mission of the organization. Jeff had planned to keep the traveling teams of volunteers "small and manageable," but from that first service project, the group grew larger and larger each year. "Not just because we were taking more first responders from New York and ground zero," Jeff explains, "and more construction workers, and more 9/11 family members and other New Yorkers who were watching people jump that day—this is their therapy—but what happened was every year people from these small towns that we previously helped on the 9/11 anniversary, every year, people from every single town kept showing up to help, to pay it forward to the next community."

A many-layered purpose developed for the foundation: expressing gratitude to those who reached out to New York after 9/11, giving New Yorkers a positive outlet to deal with the trauma of the event, rebuilding on the anniversary of a day that might otherwise only represent destruction and mourning, and providing volunteers from all over the country with opportunities to give meaning to disasters they'd experienced by paying it forward.

Jeff committed to keep the projects going for ten years, taking at least one member from every community they'd helped to work in the next community. If they could spend a decade making 9/11 a day of building together, Jeff says, "It would just be the greatest testament to the sense of resilience and compassion of the American people." Volunteers saw it a bit differently, and they let Jeff know that "New York Says Thank You" had to go on for a lot longer than ten years. Each community would want the chance to extend the same kindness to another community recovering from tragedy. As far as volunteers were concerned, there was no end in sight.

Since its formal inception in 2003, "New York Says Thank You" has carried out yearly building projects, on the anniversary of 9/11, all over the country. The specifics vary, but the outcome is always a physical representation of the power of community. The group helped restore and rebuild public structures and planted trees for tornado survivors in Utica, Illinois. In Slidell, Louisiana, the organization's volunteers rebuilt a house for the family of a six-year-old boy battling leukemia— their home was destroyed by Hurricane Katrina—but first, they rebuilt his favorite fishing dock. They also led the rebuilding of a landmark community gathering place, 140-year-old Baker Chapel, destroyed by a tornado that flattened much of DeGonia Springs, Indiana. In another tornado event, the "Mid-America Council of Boy Scouts of America" lost many of their buildings to a tornado that ripped through their Little Sioux, Iowa, camp. They also lost four young Boy Scouts. "New York Says Thank You" helped build a chapel on the foundation of the structure where the boys perished. And in Bottineau, North Dakota, volunteers lent their numbers to the construction of "Annie's House," an adaptive ski lodge where disabled children and wounded warriors learn to ski.

Along the way, the organization inspired by a father's desire to insure his sons have a legacy of more than material things launched an initiative to empower children to participate in relief, recovery, and rebuilding efforts after disasters. Through "Stars of Hope," children in devastated areas are given an outlet to heal through creative service. They turn their attention away from their own difficult situations and toward the act of serving someone else in a way that's often overlooked—by providing symbols of hope. The children paint one-foot-wide wooden stars with colorful designs and messages of love, encouragement, and faith in the promise of a brighter future. The stars decorate recovering communities all over the United States and as far away as Japan.

In another nod to its beginnings, "New York Says Thank You" launched the "9/12 Generation Project," with a mission to inspire, educate, and activate the next generation of citizens. Through the project's curriculum, young students learn about 9/11 through a focus on the spirit of service and generosity exhibited on September 12, 2001 and beyond. Older students, in middle and high school, also participate in service-learning projects. Jeff wants to shape the way children think of 9/11 and teach them the value of conscientious, engaged citizenship.

Ethan and Josh Parness, the two little boys whose argument over a toy inspired the launch of "New York Says Thank You," are now actively involved in the organization, and the ripple effect of that one idea, to send a box of toys, clothes, and coins to a little girl on the other side of the country, continues. The work of "New York Says Thank You" stands as a testament to the fact that the terrorists failed in their efforts on that sunny September day to tear apart a nation. The pain and devastation left in the wake of 9/11 will linger for generations, but this ongoing remembrance of the sense of community, the beauty of sacrifice, and the acts of one citizen at a time reaching out to help another, uniting the people of a nation and of the world on 9/12, reminds us that love and our shared humanity won out over terror. If Jeff Parness and his family have their way, that will always be the case.

Nobuyuki Kobayashi

Tohokuo, Japan

The Great East Japan Earthquake

I was having my nails done at my favorite salon one day, talking with some of the staff and clients, when the subject turned to my writing. The young woman giving me a manicure, Yumiko, suddenly said to me, "I have the perfect person for you to interview for your book!" She went on to tell me about Tokyo photographer Nobuyuki Kobayashi and the project he'd undertaken after the 2011 Japan earthquake and tsunami. Yumiko happened to be part of the team organizing an exhibition of his "3.11 Portrait Project" in Toronto the following month, and she arranged for me to meet with and interview him while he was in Canada.

I had the honor of sitting down with Mr. Kobayashi while his exhibit was on display in Toronto. Since I don't speak Japanese (although I should, considering my maternal background is Japanese-Canadian), I arranged for a translator to lead us through the interview. While I couldn't understand Mr. Kobayashi's words, his energy and spirit shone through, and I could tell his story was special.

Mr. Kobayashi gave thousands of tsunami survivors a new beginning through the transformative power of photography, helping them to heal and rebuild their lives. The portraits he took of them, some of which appear in this book, demonstrate each person's strength, courage, and resilience. I am honored to have the opportunity to share his story, and his photos, with all of you.

Nobuyuki Kobayashi, the founder of the 3/11 Project following the Japan earthquake and tsunami in 2011. (promo picture provided by Mr. Kobayashi)

A photo album lays among the debris following the 2011 Japan tsunami. Photo credit: Nobuyuki Kobayashi

A little girl reviews her image during her family's photo shoot with Nobuyuki Kobayashi. Photo credit: Nobuyuki Kobayashi

As part of the 3/11 Project, Japanese schoolchildren write and frame hand-written messages to families who lost everything following the 2011 tsunami. Photo credit: Nobuyuki Kobayashi

On a chilly day at the tail end of winter, internationally-renowned photographer Nobuyuki Kobayashi was working in his home office when the house began to shake. His first thoughts were of his wife. Where was she, and was she okay? As the tremors continued, he reached his wife and confirmed that she was safe, and then he set about finding out what exactly had happened. Japan experiences more earthquakes per year than any other country, so the event wasn't uncommon, but an Internet search revealed that this one was not like the others.

A massive earthquake had rocked the Tohoku region in the northeast. Four million homes in Tokyo, where Nobuyuki lived, were left without power, even though they were 250 miles from the earthquake's epicenter. Cell phone service was limited, and trains came to a halt, leaving commuters stranded in the city, but the damage in the capital was minimal. Nobuyuki's own home was intact, so he was stunned by images of the destruction the quake had caused in the hardest-hit areas. The scenes reminded him of the devastation of the 9/11 terrorist attacks, which he'd seen firsthand when he traveled to New York to photograph the aftermath. Through an interpreter, he explains, "I started to think, what can I do? What ideas can I come up with, and what actions can I possibly take?"

It was the afternoon of Friday, March 11, 2011, and Nobuyuki, along with millions of Japanese citizens, had just experienced what would be known as the Great East Japan Earthquake, the largest to hit the island nation in its recorded history. "Great," in this case, isn't just a vague descriptor. Seismologists use the term for earthquakes at the highest end of magnitude scales. This one registered at 9.0, making it the world's fourth largest earthquake since the Richter scale was created in 1935.

The ground buckled and shook for as long as 30 minutes in some areas, resulting in impassable roads, downed power lines, and collapsed buildings. Houses and industrial buildings went up in flames. Landslides blocked highways and crushed homes. The initial violence done by tectonic plates shifting twenty miles below the ocean's surface, eighty miles from the coast, was only the beginning.

Tsunami warnings sounded, and less than an hour after the quake, the water poured in, rushing over seawalls and breakwaters and reaching heights over thirty feet. It crashed through coastal towns and rolled as far as six miles inland. The inexorable waves swept away anything and anyone in their path. As the water receded, it left behind demolished fishing boats and mud-drenched automobiles. Where homes, shops, and schools once stood, there were now debris fields. Croplands and entire forests were wiped out.

Between the earthquake and the tsunami, more than 300,000 people were left without homes, many with no access to food, water, heat, or electricity. Thousands of survivors were injured, many trapped beneath the rubble, while strong aftershocks hindered rescue efforts. Sadly, a variety of unfortunate factors, including the underestimation of the potential size of the tsunami, conspired to prevent many residents from evacuating before the tsunami barreled through their towns. While the nature of the event made it difficult to calculate losses, in the following days, official numbers would climb to more than 15,000 dead and nearly 5,000 missing. The 24 million tons of wreckage created by the two events would take years to clear away.

Within a few weeks of the tragedy, Nobuyuki visited the disaster area at the request of a friend who urged him to come and photograph the scene. During this journey, he witnessed residents beginning to rebuild their towns, an incredibly daunting task. Seeing their focus on the future, Nobuyuki realized what part he should play. "By the evening of my first day spent in the disaster area," he says, "I already had a blueprint for the project." With more than twenty years' experience as a photographer, he wanted to use his vocation to make a difference, but Nobuyuki believed documenting the process of reconstruction was best left to photojournalists. He had in mind something more personal, an initiative focused on the emotional well-being of the survivors.

For the most part, the displaced residents lost all their possessions when their homes were destroyed, including irreplaceable photo albums filled with memories. Portraits, Nobuyuki thought, could not only provide the start of a new collection of family pictures, but the experience of posing for them could also nurture the positive spirit he believed survivors would need to sustain them as they worked to reclaim their lives. "Even if only for one moment," he explains, "I wanted them to laugh or feel a ray of hope for the future."

There was another purpose to Nobuyuki's portrait-taking mission. After the tsunami, nuclear reactor meltdowns in power plants in Fukushima Prefecture dominated headlines around the world. The reactors posed a very real threat, but the coverage eclipsed that of the daily struggles of the people who'd lost not only their homes, but their home towns, jobs, and in many cases, friends and family members. Nobuyuki's "3.11 Portrait Project" aimed to ensure that the men, women, and children who'd had so much taken from them weren't forgotten over the years it would take to rebuild their lives.

Through personal contacts and social media outreach, Nobuyuki recruited a team of top hairstylists, makeup artists, and photographers. Dozens of volunteers dedicated their weekends to putting their creativity and talents to work for the project. In preparation for their photo shoots, the survivors were pampered with hair and makeup styling. As individuals, couples, and multi-generational families, they smiled and posed in front of a white backdrop, and as they did, the weight they carried seemed to lighten. By the end of the year, more than 2,000 survivors in evacuation centers would have their portraits taken.

Photo credit: Nobuyuki Kobayashi

Photo credit: Nobuyuki Kobayashi

Photo credit: Nobuyuki Kobayashi

Photo credit: Nobuyuki Kobayashi

Photo credit: Nobuyuki Kobayashi

Photo credit: Nobuyuki Kobayashi

Photo credit: Nobuyuki Kobayashi

Photo credit: Nobuyuki Kobayashi

Photo credit: Nobuyuki Kobayashi

Photo credit: Nobuyuki Kobayashi

When asked which photo sessions hold a special place in his memory, Nobuyuki says there are too many to choose just a few, but he refers to a Japanese public television report that followed some of the "3.11 Portrait Project" stories. In the broadcast, one woman says of her time in front of the camera, "My loneliness disappeared for a moment," while a gentleman beams at his portrait and says, "This will be a stepping stone to the future." Parents lift toddlers and coaxed them to smile for the photographer, and a family holds an infant child born after the earthquake. Teenagers pose like pop stars and flash peace signs. An atmosphere of normalcy and good cheer prevails.

Later in the program, a woman wears dark sunglasses as her photo is taken. Her best friend perished in the disaster, and the shock of the whole ordeal caused the woman to lose vision in one eye. Her initial portrait captures an image of her sorrow, but with a few minutes of encouragement, her expression brightens. She removes her dark glasses and black vest and poses holding a small bouquet of daffodils. In the following days and weeks, she no longer wears the sunglasses that had kept the world at bay.

The "3.11 Portrait Project" created for the survivors a pleasant distraction from their predicament and an opportunity to share their stories with volunteers. However, Nobuyuki had a vision of something even bigger and more impactful. He reached out to schools in areas not affected by the disaster, enlisting students in elementary, middle, and high schools to frame the portraits. While they worked, the photographer shared what he'd learned of the survivors' experiences. In one classroom, the students wanted to know why a man appeared naked in his portrait. Nobuyuki explained that the man, who worked raising scallops before the Great East Japan Earthquake, took off his clothes as he posed with his family behind a banner that read "Big Catch." "Everything has been swept away," the man said. "There is nothing left. That being the case, I have nothing but my own body again. I will start up again from zero."

The students also wrote letters of consolation and encouragement to the survivors. "In this way," Nobuyuki says, "I hoped to foster a connection between individuals that would last into the future. I hoped it would help provide some support for the burden of reconstruction over the next ten to twenty years. I also felt confident that, precisely using an exchange like this, memories of the disaster would not fade."

Volunteers delivered the portraits and the accompanying letters to the survivors, and Nobuyuki says, "Handing over the photographs to the families was a main part of the project, and many of them were overjoyed. There were many people who started crying as soon as they saw the photographs." Several people were so moved by the students' letters that they wrote back to express their gratitude, striking up an ongoing correspondence with the young people, much to Nobuyuki's delight.

When project volunteers returned months later to visit, grateful residents waited outside their temporary homes to greet them. "Even when it was snowing, there were people who would wait for us like this," says Nobuyuki. He stays in touch with a number of the people he photographed and plans to return to document some of their special occasions and major life events, but cognizant of local photographers' need to rebuild their businesses, Nobuyuki brought the portrait-taking phase of the project to a close.

"What I wanted to do," says Nobuyuki, "is not only to be confined to Japan but rather to widen the circle of caring as much as possible." To accomplish this, he created a traveling exhibition of the "3.11 Portrait Project," which so far has been displayed in Japan, Canada, Finland, France, and the United States. Through his work, the survivors' stories are passed on, and Nobuyuki Kobayashi's spirit of optimism, solidarity, and compassion goes with them.

Bob and Fonda Walsh

New Orleans, Louisiana

Hurricane Katrina

I met Bob and Fonda Walsh through Bob Nakao, the organizer of "Continuity Cares," when I was part of a team tasked with gutting and rebuilding the home of one of their employees, Stanley Meyers. His house had been destroyed by Hurricane Katrina, and Stanley had recently been diagnosed with terminal cancer. The Walshes wanted to ensure he and his family could enjoy the last years of his life back in the familiar warmth of their family home.

The project provided me with an opportunity to talk at length with Bob and Fonda at Stanley's house, and I was moved by how concerned and committed they were to their employees and their well-being. This was no ordinary company; this was family.

After the hurricane, the couple used their business as a resource to make rebuilding a life in New Orleans a real possibility for their employees. Bob and Fonda Walsh are remarkable people. They're also remarkable business owners, a husband-and-wife team, who together, truly deserve the title of "World's Greatest Boss."

Bob and Fonda Walsh with Stanley Meyers in front of his home in New Orleans, LA in 2007. The Walshes helped rebuild Stanley's home after it was destroyed by Hurricane Katrina. Photo credit: Suzanne Bernier

In a disaster of the magnitude of the one created by Hurricane Katrina, there is no greater tragedy than the loss of life; as a result of the 2005 storm, more than 1,800 people died. In addition, more than a million people in the Gulf region were displaced, and many of them would never return. At the same time, hundreds of thousands of domesticated animals struggled to survive on their own, and many of them also died in the disaster. The Federal Emergency Management Agency (FEMA) deemed the event "the single most catastrophic natural disaster and costliest hurricane in U.S. history."

Dramatic statistics like these illustrate very real losses and challenges, but they also overshadow another kind of loss that profoundly impacts individuals, families, and communities. When businesses of all kinds close their doors in the wake of disaster, the people left unemployed must deal with a sense of uncertainty about their financial futures and the stress of not knowing how they'll meet their most basic expenses. The quick action and altruism of volunteers and relief organizations provide invaluable resources, but survivors don't want to remain dependent on such assistance for any longer than necessary. A return to work offers them the beginning of a return to normalcy.

Within months of the devastation brought to pass by Hurricane Katrina, the levee failure, and the ensuing flood, the U.S. Labor Department would report that the storm resulted in the disappearance of more than 230,000 jobs. For small business owners Bob and Fonda Walsh, the idea that their company's more than 100 employees would be left without means to provide for themselves and their families proved unacceptable.

The Walshes initially planned to ride out the storm in their North Shore home, but after watching televised images of Katrina closing in on the Gulf Coast with sustained winds of 220 miles per hour, they decided to err on the side of caution. On Monday, August 29, 2005, the couple packed up and drove to Hot Springs, Arkansas, where they spent the night in a hotel. But they were anxious to know how things were back at home, and after learning the storm had passed, they decided to return early the next morning.

As they sped by closed gas stations and dark restaurants, theirs was the only vehicle headed south, and Bob started to have doubts about going back so soon. When he shared his hesitation with his wife, she wouldn't hear of postponing their return. Fonda told him, "Keep driving. We're going home."

Local officials bombarded radio airwaves with warnings for residents who'd reached safe haven to stay away, but Bob and Fonda wouldn't be deterred. They felt a responsibility to find out what New Orleans and the surrounding areas were up against, and along the way, they discovered local residents weren't just sitting around waiting for help to arrive. Many had started clearing the back roads the Walshes traveled on their journey home, and while downed trees littered the main entrance to their subdivision, the developer already had workers laboring to make it passable.

Fonda and Bob found their ranch, and the cows and horses they'd been forced to leave behind, all in good shape. However, there was no electricity, and so, no air conditioning. The late summer Louisiana heat bore down on them relentlessly, motivating them to find a better place to stay in the short term, but such comforts were far from their top priority. They immediately set about getting Gulf Coast Office Products, the company Bob Walsh founded with his partner, Bill Kenny, in 1977, back in business.

At the time, Gulf Coast had two offices, one in New Orleans, which was inaccessible due to the flooding in the city, and another in Baton Rouge. Bob and Fonda headed to the second site, where the damage was much less extensive. Their newer office turned out to be in a part of the city that still had electrical power, and they laid out a plan to get back to work as quickly as possible.

Bob sought out his banker so he could have cash on hand for employees who might need an advance or a loan to get reestablished, though few would take him up on the offer. Certain that employees would have the same instinct to come home that had driven her and her husband to return, Fonda looked for hotel rooms to rent for them, but vacancies were in short supply. Luckily, she came across a house being prepared for sale and was able to rent it. She recalls, "It basically had no furniture, but it was a huge house. …We had some sleeping bags, and everybody just put together whatever they could put together, but nobody complained because there were no hotels."

Some of the company's workers and their families stayed in the house for up to six months while they waited for insurance payouts and the renovation of houses flooded with ten to twelve feet of water. And when the company's warehouse delivery manager was diagnosed with cancer shortly after the natural disaster, and underwent surgery which prevented him from working, the Walshes stepped up to pay for all the supplies needed to rebuild his family's home.

The wheels of restoration turned quickly for Gulf Coast Office Products and the people who made it run. As warehouse workers, delivery drivers, salespeople, and office personnel called in and learned Bob and Fonda were getting things up and running, more of them trickled back into town.

Shortly after they started reorganizing to move their center of operations to Baton Rouge, Bob answered the office phone to find a representative from FEMA on the line. "They ordered a million dollars' worth of equipment from me over the phone," he says. When he asked the representative why they'd called his company instead of one of the nationally-known alternatives in the area, Bob learned that Gulf Coast wasn't the first office supply provider FEMA tried to contract with. On the contrary, they'd called other companies, but the calls went unanswered. "We were the only ones with electricity," says Bob.

That FEMA order for office equipment proved to be the Walshes' ticket back into the city of New Orleans. Because they were now working for the federal government, Gulf Coast employees were issued passes allowing them to enter the city, and while their New Orleans office had sustained some damage, Bob and Fonda discovered that everything they needed to run their business—servers, computers, and backup equipment—was still in perfect working order.

Around the same time, the couple found out that their purchasing and inventory specialist, Carol, was still in town. She'd had a baby two weeks earlier and weathered the storm in a local hospital, where her young child had been readmitted for a minor health issue while the rest of her family evacuated. But when the hospital told Carol she and the baby would have to be discharged, she made her way to an evacuation center. A woman visiting the center saw the infant and felt moved to invite the little family of two to stay with her in her home.

Fonda secured a hotel room for Carol, but the woman hosting her insisted Carol and the baby continue to be her guests. The two women, who'd never crossed paths before the hurricane, developed a lasting friendship, and with a suitable place to live, Carol went back to work for Gulf Coast Office Products. "Now we had our computer system, our purchasing inventory lady, our delivery trucks, and our salespeople," says Fonda. "So we were in business."

Believing New Orleans would be inaccessible for quite some time, the two large national office supply competitors with a presence in the area pulled out of the region. As businesses put together whatever they could to get back to normal operations as soon as possible, restoring their offices or setting up in less affected areas nearby, Gulf Coast was the only game in town to fulfill their office supply needs. Deliveries scheduled for New Orleans were rerouted to Baton Rouge and business flourished as more employees came back to their jobs. "The ones that came back, we made sure they were okay, that they were ready to work," says Fonda. "They didn't want a handout. They just wanted a salary."

One salesman, whose family lost everything in the flood, showed up at the office but wouldn't come inside. Accustomed to wearing a suit and tie every day to meet with large account customers, like the New Orleans Saints, it embarrassed him to be seen walking around the office wearing a pair of shorts.

Reflecting on a state of mind difficult for people who've never experienced it to understand, Fonda says, "These were people who lived in New Orleans all their lives, and when they got ready to evacuate, even knowing the seriousness of it, they didn't take anything. Everybody assumes, as many times as they've evacuated, that it won't happen this time."

But "it" did happen this time. Most of the employees of Gulf Coast Office Products lost their homes, and the security of a steady paycheck proved invaluable in helping them rebuild their lives after Hurricane Katrina. It can never be easy to recover from such a disaster, but in this case, the combination of an unyielding work ethic, good fortune, and well-earned loyalty on both sides coalesced to transform the tragedy for more than 100 people and the families that depended on them.

In the face of disaster, it can be easy to overlook the ways a shutdown of commerce can aggravate what are already the most trying circumstances. The Walshes recognized the importance of survivors having a purpose, earning their keep, and receiving the chance to take responsibility for the rebuilding of their own lives.

As a direct result of Fonda and Bob's efforts to ensure the safety and stability of their employees, they were ultimately rewarded for their efforts with record profits the following year.

Little did they know that, just by doing the right thing, their company would flourish after Katrina, having inherited business from competitors who had no staff, no customers, and no way to remain open following the disaster. In the end, their efforts, and the efforts of the scores of people working for their company, were greatly rewarded in ways they never could have imagined.

Dennise McIntyre

Slave Lake, Alberta

The Slave Lake Fire

Canada has, of course, faced many emergencies over the years, but our country has been extremely fortunate. We haven't experienced many large-scale disasters that resulted in numerous deaths and injuries. However, incidents like the Lac-Mégantic train derailment, the Calgary floods, and the Eastern Canada ice storm remind us that no community is immune to disaster. We have our own share of disasters and heroes, right here at home.

Karina Pillay Kinnee, mayor of Slave Lake at the time of the 2011 Slave Lake wildfire, passed Dennise McIntyre's name on to me. After doing some research online, I found out Dennise, a local pet groomer, was responsible for organizing a rescue and saving the lives of hundreds of household pets while her entire community evacuated to escape a deadly wildfire that roared through the town.

Dennise agreed to share her story, which highlights the importance of "pet planning" during emergencies. If you were asked to evacuate your home within six hours, would you be prepared to bring your pet or pets with you? If so, how would you transport and house them? If not, where would they go and how would they get there? Does your community or a neighboring community have kennels identified and available during an emergency?

Luckily for the residents of Slave Lake, Alberta, Dennise McIntyre jumped into action to save the lives of those who couldn't save themselves—the beloved animals whose families had to outrun the fire without them.

What happens to the pets—dogs and cats, parakeets and hamsters, gerbils and reptiles—left behind when a large-scale disaster forces a town's entire population to evacuate with little notice? It's a question those on the outside looking in often consider as an afterthought, but for people like Dennise McIntyre, the welfare of animals is never far from top of mind. A lifelong animal lover, dog groomer by profession, and devoted animal welfare advocate, Dennise lives her life on the outskirts of Slave Lake, Alberta, with a deep commitment to the care and protection of animals.

With sandy beaches and plentiful fishing, surrounded by thousands of acres of forests teaming with wildlife from beavers to bears and elk, and Marten Mountain beckoning hikers with promises of stunning views, Slave Lake is a nature lover's dream. After relocating in 2000 from Calgary to the neighborhood of Widewater just outside Slave Lake, Dennise lived what might be considered a typical small-town lifestyle. Her sister and parents lived nearby, and as her two daughters grew into adulthood and started their own families, they remained in the area. While raising their youngest child, Cody, Dennise and her husband, Roy, worked in town, and as a local business owner, Dennise was well-known and respected among other business owners and the community at large.

Dennise divided her time between home, her pet grooming shop, and her work on behalf of the nonprofit Animal Rescue Committee of Slave Lake. As the organization's president, Dennise worked with the town to replace its rundown dog pound with a new animal holding facility. She also managed a system of foster homes for stray and abandoned pets, with the ultimate goal of placing the animals in permanent adoptive homes.

On the afternoon of Saturday, May 14, 2011, the quiet life enjoyed by the McIntyres and Slave Lake's seven thousand residents was disrupted when a fire started near the town and officials declared a state of emergency. Wildfires are fairly common in the area, and initially, firefighters believed they could contain the blaze and protect the town. Still, Dennise was concerned that if the fire spread quickly they wouldn't have much time to evacuate. She recalls telling her husband, "I think we better move the horses. I have this gut feeling that something's going to happen, and we aren't going to be able to get up there in time for them." Acting on her instinct, they transported several horses and ponies, along with the steer and heifer Cody was raising as his 4-H project, to a location not likely to be affected by the fire.

Dennise's concerns proved spot on. High winds and extreme dry conditions fueled the fire, and by Sunday afternoon, it had burned through almost five thousand acres and was moving in the direction of Widewater. Spending the day in town, the McIntyres learned their neighborhood was being evacuated, and they rushed back to Widewater with just an hour or two to grab what they could from their home and the home of Dennise's parents. Pets in tow, they settled in town at the house Dennise and Roy's younger daughter, Tamara, owned with her boyfriend, Jesse.

The family waited there, hoping the firefighters would be able to stop the wildfire from advancing. They learned the fire had jumped to the town proper when they saw the house across the street going up in flames. With a growing sense of panic, they moved quickly to get family members and all their pets back in their cars and trucks, but there was one problem. Dennise's sister, Bonnie, was already out of town, and unfortunately, her two huskies, Maggie and Charlie, were too big to fit in the packed vehicles. Low on options, Jesse kicked down the gate to give the dogs a chance to escape the fire on their own. "You're thinking, just let them run, and we'll find them later," says Dennise. Huskies are renowned for their endurance, and the dogs would have no problem running for miles, but there was always the risk that they'd choose a wrong direction and end up trapped by the fire. There was simply no other choice. Maggie and Charlie would have to flee the looming danger on their own.

The going was slow as hundreds of residents attempted to leave that side of town at the same time. Two men tried to move things along by directing traffic, but the fire was so close, embers singed their hair, and they choked and gagged on the heavy smoke and ash filling the air. Roy and Tamara were forced to abandon their vehicles and everything in them and ride with other family members, but eventually, the caravan of evacuees made its way to the other side of town, and Dennise secured her dogs and cats at the grooming shop.

Without cellular phone service it took some time to reunite everyone, and not long after the family was back together, all of Slave Lake was ordered to evacuate. The McIntyre family prepared to head out of town, but officials asked Roy to stay behind. As the manager of an equipment rental shop, he had access to resources, like light towers and generators, that the town needed, and he agreed to stay and help. Dennise says she couldn't bring herself to leave without her husband. It's a part of her story she can't tell without choking up. "I told my kids, you go," she says, "because I'm not leaving without your dad. They didn't want to do it, but I had to force them." She kept two large dogs with her while family members took the smaller dogs. The animals sheltered at the grooming shop were taken to a safer location, but two of Dennise's cats couldn't be found in the hasty move and were left behind.

As they drove through town, Dennise and Roy witnessed houses burning unchecked, and as Dennise had feared, Tamara and Jesse's house was one of them. Roy spent the rest of the night supporting the firefighting effort, and after getting a few hours of sleep at a nearby friend's house, he and Dennise returned to Slave Lake early the next morning. While Roy went back to work supplying equipment, Dennise fed and watered the animals and checked to see if her grooming shop had survived the night. Fortunately, the building hadn't suffered any fire damage, and to her relief, she discovered one of her two missing cats sleeping inside.

By that afternoon, the main fires had been extinguished, but with public services such as running water and electricity scarce, and high winds threatening to spread the spot fires that lingered among the trees, the evacuation order was upheld. Dennise rode along with a peace officer through streets where buildings untouched by the fire stood next to spots where structures had been reduced to ashes. Burned out shells of cars littered neighborhood roads, and much of the lush, verdant landscape surrounding the town was now a barren scene of charred tree trunks. Dennise crossed paths with a police officer who told her about dogs stranded on balconies in town, and soon after, the fire department called to see if she could care for a cat that had been badly singed.

Realizing there were likely many more pets left on their own, most without access to food and water, Dennise began to think of how she could launch an animal rescue. When representatives of the Edmonton Humane Society connected with her and offered to deploy volunteers to assist in whatever ways they could, her plan came together. Dennise and her team would retrieve the animals, and the humane society would transport them out of Slave Lake, but Dennise still needed to assemble her team. She put in a call for help to the vice chairperson of the Animal Rescue Committee of Slave Lake.

Vanessa Bjornson and her husband left their young child with relatives and came back to help Dennise carry out the pet rescue. As word spread about Dennise's plan, more volunteers returned to join the effort, including Tamara and Jesse, who, even after learning they'd lost their home, insisted on coming back to lend a hand. The number of volunteers reached a total of about twenty people, and with the help of her small team, Dennise set up a temporary holding facility for the animals in a part of town that still had electrical power.

Dennise McIntyre, Chairperson & Vanessa Bjornson, Vice-Chairperson of the Animal Rescue Committee of Slave Lake.

Group photo of some of the rescue team from the Animal Rescue Committee of Slave Lake and Edmonton Humane Society.

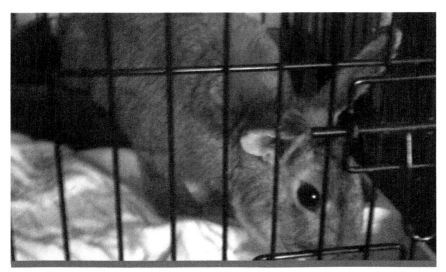

Rescued bunny waiting to be transported to Athabasca or Edmonton holding facility for family to pick up following the 2011 Slave Lake wildfire. Photo credit: Vanessa Bjornson

Waiting to be transported to Athabasca or Edmonton holding facility for family to pick up. Photo credit: Vanessa Bjornson

Photo credit: Vanessa Bjornson

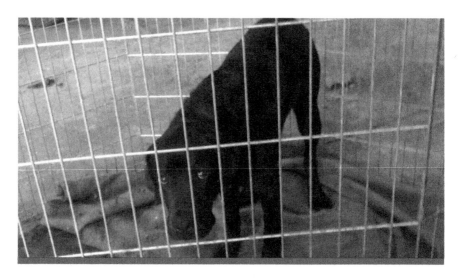

Waiting to be transported to Athabasca or Edmonton holding facility for family to pick up. Photo credit: Vanessa Bjornson

First staging area at the Town of Slave Lake Maintenance Shop. Photo credit: Vanessa Bjornson

Aaron Bjornson, an ARC rescue team member, looking at what is left of his sister's home. Photo credit: Vanessa Bjornson

The animal rescue team's second staging area. Photo credit: Vanessa Bjornson

Photo credit: Vanessa Bjornson

The group publicized their contact information on local news shows and on the humane society's website, encouraging townspeople to call and let them know about any animals that needed to be retrieved from vacated homes. Two tech-savvy volunteers created an online system to identify the animals and match them to their owners, and the humane society set up dispatch centers in Athabasca and Edmonton, where most residents waited for the chance to return home. When pet owners called, they could request their pets be transported to either site.

As the media picked up the story of the work Dennise and her team were doing, animal lovers sent in donations to support the effort. Animal Rescue Committee of Slave Lake typically operated on a small budget, so the money was appreciated and put to good use, but it was also an added responsibility to manage. Then there were the demands of the media to contend with. Dennise says, "Because I was the main person in the group, they wanted to interview me. Well, it was pretty overwhelming. You haven't showered for three days or whatever, and you're trying to keep it together." Stephanie McDonald, the executive director of Edmonton Humane Society, stepped up to handle all media requests for interviews and information, freeing Dennise to focus on, and participate in, the rescues.

In teams of two, volunteers went from home to home, and when necessary, a police officer or locksmith helped them gain entry. Once inside, they calmed and coaxed anxious animals and brought them to the temporary shelter. Some of the more challenging assignments involved frightened pets that hid in cluttered homes and resisted being taken away from the one place they felt safe—moments which could easily turn comical, as three or four people struggled to get their hands on one nervous cat or bird—but the team managed to carry off hundreds of rescues without injury to themselves or to any of the animals. Dennise says the hardest moments were those when they arrived too late. "There were a couple of dogs who wouldn't leave the property, and they succumbed to the fire," she explains. "There was that kind of devastation."

Fortunately, most of the efforts were carried out in a fairly routine manner, and the team brought in any pet they could safely shelter. "We had rabbits and birds, and cats and dogs, of course, chinchillas, the caged animals, gerbils, guinea pigs, all kinds of different things," recounts Dennise. "We had a guy call in and say he had over seventy snakes." In that case, they made special arrangements with the police to have the snake breeder escorted by Dennise and two team members, so he could handle the reptiles himself.

Some residents preferred that their pets be left where they were, but asked the volunteers to replenish the animals' food and water, so the team needed a way to distinguish the animals that weren't to be removed from their homes. Team members identified themselves by wearing yellow bandanas, and they used the same marker to indicate an animal that should be left in place. Dennise explains, "We would tie [a yellow bandana] on a tree in front of that house, meaning this one is being looked after. Don't take the animals."

Meanwhile, Bonnie's huskies were still running loose, though one of them, Charlie, was seen around town on several occasions. Charlie appeared to be in good shape, but made skittish by all the upheaval, she refused to let anyone bring her in. When officers told Dennise they'd spotted the dog in a residential area, she grabbed a couple of leashes and rushed out to see if Charlie would trust someone familiar. Instead, Dennise happened upon the other husky, Maggie, and brought her back to the shelter.

While she was thrilled to recover one of her sister's beloved dogs, Dennise asked everyone to give up the attempts to bring Charlie home. Instead, she left food and water in Bonnie's yard, about five miles outside of town, and as she suspected would happen, a few days later, Charlie turned up there. Both huskies had made it back to their family, and Dennise reunited Charlie and Maggie and cared for the dogs until she could return them to her sister.

As the animal rescue continued, a volunteer put out traps to catch and bring in any cats straying about town. A few days into the evacuation, he set a trap in front of Dennise's shop, and the next morning, Dennise found her missing cat there. The animal was exhausted, with minor injuries from trying to escape the trap, but alive and well. Dennise remembers the moment with a palpable sense of joy because, with that discovery, every one of the family's pets was safe and accounted for. They'd all survived the fire.

In one happy reunion after another, residents claimed their pets at the dispatch centers. The singed cat that inspired the animal rescue effort healed quickly and was one of the first to reunite with its owners. It turned out the cat belonged to the family of a mechanic who worked for Roy. A Rottweiler that had wandered into the fire department and settled in for the duration was identified by its owners, although by then, the firefighters had grown attached to the dog and wanted to adopt it as their mascot. They were sorry to see the dog go, but the two children he belonged with were anxious to have Moose back. Another resident was so grateful to have his cat and dog safely returned to him, he started a fundraiser selling "I love Slave Lake" T-shirts and raised $30,000, money he divided between the fire department and the Animal Rescue Committee of Slave Lake.

Entire subdivisions burned to the ground in the Slave Lake fire, which after a lengthy investigation, was linked to arson. In total, more than four hundred homes and other structures were lost, and while Dennise and Roy's home was spared, like Tamara and Jesse, Dennise's parents lost their house and everything in it. With the exception of a pilot who crashed while fighting the fire from the air, there were no human casualties. While many people expected the evacuation to last at least a month, town officials had public services up and running and the evacuation order lifted within two weeks.

Dennise and her band of volunteers rescued and cared for more than three hundred pets, most of which would otherwise have perished from starvation or dehydration. For many residents who lost all or most of their worldly possessions, the knowledge that their pets survived the fire provided a lifeline of hope in a time of turmoil and uncertainty. For that bit of solace, Dennise McIntyre deserves much of the credit. With the fire behind them, Dennise and the volunteers of the Animal Rescue Committee of Slave Lake continue their work caring for animals and raising funds to finance the construction of a humane, state-of-the-art shelter to house abandoned and homeless pets. The new building will be disaster-ready.

Scott Lewis

Republic of Haiti

The 2010 Haiti Earthquake

Scott Lewis, sometimes referred to as Florida's "Landscaper to the Stars," is a perfect example of how, with faith and determination, the skills developed for a completely different purpose can be transferred after a disaster and be used to make a huge difference and even to save lives. Scott did just that when he and his small team fed tens of thousands of people who would otherwise have faced starvation after a disaster left them with no access to food.

I met with Scott in the spring of 2013 at his office in West Palm Beach, Florida. He spent the day sharing stories, photos, and memories of his time commanding food distribution operations in Haiti in the immediate aftermath of the 2010 earthquake that devastated that nation. Scott has taken part in many other disaster relief efforts since, and at the time of this writing, is back in Haiti helping to rebuild.

Learning about the positive impact Scott had on the lives of survivors, under incredibly challenging circumstances, had a profound effect on me. I was so inspired by him, his efforts, and the disaster organization he has since founded, that I signed up to be one of his volunteers.

Thousands of people deep, the throng of starving earthquake survivors rushed the three men who stood between them and the food distribution center, crushing the trio against the gates of the compound. One of the trapped men, a Haitian National Police officer, swung his cane to try and hold back the crowd, and another, an armed guard, did his best to ward off the wave of people threatening to trample them.

The third man, Scott Lewis, a business owner from Florida, had come out of the compound to try to restore order. Now he felt the outline of a shotgun imprinted in his back as he slammed against one of the men charged with protecting him. Scott looked around for any sign of help and cast his hopes on a passing truck filled with United Nations troops.

Above the fray, a photographer perched on a wall waved for the truck to stop, dropping his camera in the process. To Scott's dismay, one truck and then another drove by without as much as slowing down to see what was happening. Gunfire rang out, but Scott's immediate concern was the very real threat of being crushed to death.

The idea that a landscaper from the Sunshine State would find himself in such a predicament seems a stretch, but the journey that led Scott to that perilous moment started eleven years earlier when he was recruited to help in his first major disaster relief effort. The Incident Command System experience Scott had garnered during his time with the Volunteer Fire Service left him with a unique skill set, and in 1999, a fire service colleague called on him to put those skills to use. He needed someone to fly down to the Bahamas and train their volunteer firefighters after the country was hit by Hurricane Floyd. He promised Scott a quick return home, and Scott agreed to go.

Once he landed in the Bahamas, Scott realized things were much worse than he'd gathered from news coverage, but he had a job to do and he set about doing it. Impressed by the depth of his expertise and his leadership capabilities the people in charge asked him to stay longer than he'd originally intended. Scott was appointed the Incident Commander for the relief operation, and what was supposed to be a one-day stint turned into a two-week assignment. The experience would set him on a tremendously rewarding, if unanticipated, path.

While Scott was serving in the islands, people back in the United States looked for ways to contribute to the effort, and many sent money. It would seem like the most effective way to help, but a $10,000 donation was stolen before it could serve its intended purpose. Dismayed by the loss, Scott decided to do something to safeguard the contributions and ensure they went to those who needed them most, rather than lining the pockets of thieves or con artists taking advantage of an easily exploited situation. He established a nonprofit foundation to properly handle the funds.

"We needed to form 'Eagles Wings,'" says Scott, "because we wanted people to know they can donate money." He took the name for the "Eagles Wings Foundation" from Isaiah 40:31, in the Old Testament of the Bible: "But those who hope in the Lord will renew their strength. They will soar on wings like eagles." He envisioned a faith-based organization that would reach beyond religious differences and bring together people of Jewish, Islamic, and Christian faiths. Scott describes the foundation's purpose as "getting an area from an emergency room into a recovery ward." Their volunteers, referred to as Pathfinders, would deliver emergency relief supplies to survivors who couldn't reach distribution points, help governments and charitable organizations coordinate relief efforts, and organize mass feeding operations.

After he finished his work in the Bahamas, Scott returned to his normal life, running Scott Lewis Gardening in Palm Beach, Florida. Periodically, The Eagle Wings Foundation was called on to respond to other disasters. And then, on Tuesday, January 12, 2010, at 4:53

p.m., a magnitude 7.0 earthquake struck the island of Hispaniola. The epicenter was located near the Haitian capital of Port-au-Prince, and the Republic of Haiti suffered one of the most catastrophic disasters in modern history.

Scott was at work when he heard the news. Details were hard to verify, but one of his senior employees, Felix Jean-Baptiste, had a connection with the police chief of Port-au-Prince. Felix lost family members and a house he owned in Haiti when the earthquake hit, and he kept Scott informed of how bad things were for the nation that struggled with extreme poverty, insufficient resources, and an unstable economy before the disaster.

By all accounts, the losses were massive. According to the Haitian government, more than 316,000 people were killed. Another 300,000 suffered injuries in the earthquake, and 1.5 million Haitians were left without shelter when more than 280,000 houses were damaged or destroyed. In a country where the majority of the population lived on less than $2 a day, material damages reached the billions.

Two days after the earthquake, Felix connected Scott with the police chief. "He requested us to come down with a small team," says Scott. Normally, the Eagles Wings Foundation would wait for a formal, written request. However, the World Food Programme, which had a presence in Haiti before the disaster, echoed the call for assistance, and Scott knew they couldn't delay their deployment.

The next day, a team of eight people, including Scott and Felix, boarded a plane bound for Port-au-Prince. Before they could land, the airport in the capital city closed to incoming flights, and they were rerouted to Santo Domingo, in the Dominican Republic. "Which was a good thing for us," says Scott, "because it let us really stock up heavy with supplies." They chartered a hotel bus and began the treacherous journey across the border and into Haiti.

Scott says, "I can remember distinctly us fording a river in the

Hilton bus because the bridge had collapsed." The mission wouldn't get any easier for some time. They reached a United Nations base at the airport, but after spending one night sleeping in tents on the tarmac, Scott knew the arrangement wouldn't work. The noise of military planes landing all night meant no one got a full night's rest. Without a place to sleep, the team's ability to function would quickly deteriorate.

After partnering with a local faith-based organization, the Pathfinders found a more suitable location for their home base, set up a communications system, stocked their own food and water supply, and located a generator. With these necessities in place, it was time to take on their first assignment, a mass feeding operation in the city of Carrefour. Even with mass care experience in the Bahamas and in post-Katrina New Orleans, this operation would test Scott and his small team in new ways. Carrefour was fast becoming one of the most dangerous places in the country.

The volunteers rounded up twenty small dump trucks to transport their bulk food supplies and brought on locals to help prepare for the distribution. While most of the team worked to organize the trucks, Scott and a couple of volunteers went out to do reconnaissance, one of the first steps on any mission. They hired a car and went off into the city, driving through a devastated commercial district, where they eventually got out to walk around and take a closer look at things. Hundreds of people milled about with no sign of trouble.

Observing the scene, Scott noticed a dust cloud a few blocks down the road. Felix saw it too. "We have to go," he said. "We have to go now!"

A group of police officers jumped in their trucks and sped away as thousands of people, many of whom brandished homemade weapons, headed right at them. Back in the car, the men did a quick U-turn, but the mob bore down on them, banging on the vehicle as it tried to get away. For Scott, it was a clear and frightening image of the desperation of a people deprived of food and running water for days. "It's worse than you could ever imagine," says Scott. Somehow, they made it out of the thick of the crowd unscathed and without running over anyone.

With the immediate threat behind them, Scott set about finding a suitable location for their first food distribution. The site would have to be secure and controllable, and a fenced hotel compound promised exactly what they needed. Distributing up to one hundred tons of food to thousands of earthquake survivors seemed doable. After all, they'd successfully completed similar missions on a smaller scale.

The team set up inside the two-acre compound, behind eight-foot walls secured by steel gates. Even before they could publicize the distribution, a line of people seeking food began to form. As the news that food had arrived spread by word of mouth, the trickle of people swelled to thousands.

For an hour and a half, things went smoothly, but as they neared the last of their food supply, Scott could see things devolving in the area just outside the gate. People were getting impatient, angry, and afraid they wouldn't receive their share of the food. Hoping to head off a potential problem, Scott went out to try and bring things back under control, a task that proved impossible.

And that's how Scott Lewis found himself fighting for his life, nearly crushed by a crowd of thousands against the gates that stood between them and the food they desperately needed. "We believe in miracles," Scott has said of his wife and himself, and they have good reason to believe. "The three of us got back inside the gate somehow," he says. "I don't really remember how."

They were back inside the compound, but the safety of the walls was just an illusion. The gates wouldn't hold. Wielding canes and sticks, a group of survivors knocked down the steel gates. Scott says, "We just backed off and let them come in. They came from everywhere at once, [even] over the walls."

Heavy gunfire from local gangs continued as people poured in, and the Eagles Wings team retreated to a courtyard, surrounded by their small band of armed security guards. They stood aside as the people grabbed what food they could. Finally, the Haitian National Police arrived in two United Nations armored personnel carriers and extracted the team from the chaotic scene.

The Pathfinders had come to an area no one else was serving because that's where they were needed, but the risks were too great. Scott wasn't prepared to work under such volatile conditions, and he couldn't jeopardize his team like that again. Their safety had to remain his first priority, and he asked to be reassigned someplace more stable. Coordinators responded by informing him that his team had fed 18,000 people that day—people who had no other hope of finding anything to eat. They had to find a way to make it work wherever they were needed, Scott decided. The mission was too important to abandon.

Even though they dramatically increased the number of troops guarding their operation, there was never enough personnel to control crowds numbering up to 30,000 people at a time. The food supply ran low as they neared the end of each distribution, and by that time, the impromptu gangs forming in the line would rush in and take what they could by force. Scott and his team implemented a system to deal with what they saw as an inevitability.

"You've got anywhere from sixty to one hundred tons of food," Scott explains. "You distribute ninety-five percent of it, and you still have 10,000 people waiting for food, and they're going to be desperate." As they reached that point, volunteers blew the whistles provided to each team member, a signal to load up the trucks and move out. They left the last of the food to those who could manage to claim it.

Scott Lewis and the Pathfinders team were assigned to mass feeding operations by the United Nations World Food Programme (WFP) to high-profile, unsecured sites like this one, in front of the Haitian National Palace, requiring complex advanced planning for each distribution. Photo credit: Jeff Waycott

This first distribution by Pathfinders at Carrefour was a distribution to over 19,000 people. However, while Pathfinders had hired 20 armed security guards for this first mission, it was not enough, and the team had to be rescued at the end of its first mission following heavy gunfire in a coordinated assault by local gangs. Photo credit: Ed Minyard

The 8-person Pathfinders team also split up distribution points like this site in Fermat to maximize the impact of their distributions, which totaled 2,467,000 meal rations in just 8 days. Photo credit: Ed Minyard

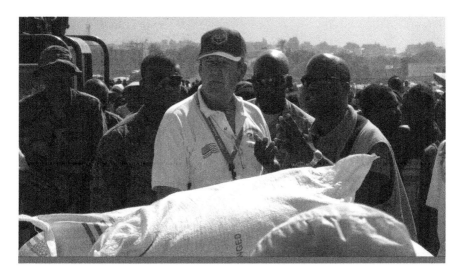

Scott Lewis consulting with Local NGO's, who proved essential in helping guide the Pathfinders' efforts like in Delmas, where Pathfinders distributed food to over 20,000 people in an open field. Photo credit: Jeff Waycott

The Pathfinder team made daily pickups from this heavily damaged World Food Programme storage facility opposite Cité Soleil. Photo credit: Ed Minyard

Scott Lewis led a small Pathfinder team to an extremely remote distribution near Ganthier which had not seen any foreign assistance at all until the team's arrival. Photo credit: Juan Godoy

Croix du Bouquet was one of the most successful mass feeding operations by Pathfinders, with 12,400 people collecting mixed bags of food in just 40 minutes. Photo credit: Colonel Dave Larivee

The 20-truck convoys of Pathfinders were easily identifiable as they snaked through Port-au-Prince to avoid travel challenges throughout the city. Photo credit: Colonel Dave Larivee

Breaking down the World Food Programme's bulk food into 25-pound sacks with oil, salt, beans, and rice took teams all night to sort in preparation for the next day's distributions. Photo credit: Colonel Dave Larivee

On its fourth tasking following the earthquake, Pathfinders worked under Handicap International and distributed more than 30,000 meal rations donated by the City of New Orleans. Here, local Pathfinder Berdy Brenovil teaches orphans how to make a hot meal. Photo credit: Colonel Dave Larivee

After a few days, the Pathfinders discovered another way to better manage crowd control. By deploying lengths of barbed wire, they were able to funnel people through the distribution process in a more orderly manner. By the final day of the mission, they had a system in place that allowed them to feed 12,400 people in 40 minutes—and without the melee that ended each of the earlier distributions.

Scott credits Air Force Colonel Dave LaRivee, who received special leave to assist the Pathfinders, with lending them the expertise they needed to reach that level of efficiency. From that first experience in Haiti, the foundation developed a process to distribute emergency meal rations at an average of 10,000 people an hour. Scott also points out that the local volunteers from faith-based organizations and other survivors consistently provided invaluable hours of labor, without which the job couldn't have gotten done.

On the second day of operations, distributions in open fields near Cité Soleil were difficult at best.

After feeding upwards of 100,000 people on that first seven-day trip, the team returned to Haiti on several more deployments, and Scott had opportunities to work more closely with Haitian citizens. On one trip, they participated in the rehabilitation of the National General Hospital, restoring the emergency room building to working condition. They also coordinated the installation of a satellite communications system, which allows hospital personnel to consult with medical experts in other parts of the world. On another trip, they brought relief supplies to an organization that worked with the disabled, delivering everything from crutches and wheelchairs to shoes and MREs.

While working with a group of nonprofits to set up basic health and sanitation facilities, they stumbled on scores of children living in an auto junkyard. The boys and girls huddled behind a wall of old cars, hungry and afraid. With the assistance of a local church group, Scott's team relocated the children to one of the orphanages that sprung up after the earthquake left tens of thousands of children without parents to care for them. For Scott, seeing the children in a safe, welcoming environment was a special kind of reward. "I don't know where these kids were sleeping the night before we found them," he says. "I do know that the night after we found them, they were in houses."

As Scott describes his experience with the orphans, he's reminded of a moment from that first, harrowing deployment to Haiti. In the darkness of night, he, Felix, and their driver drove less than five-miles-an-hour down a narrow road so pitted with pot holes that to go any faster was to risk a broken axle. As they inched on, out of nowhere people began to stream alongside them. Within minutes, thousands of people filled the road, surrounding their car.

After barely surviving two previous encounters with rioting crowds of survivors, alarm bells went off for Scott. The group pulled over to assess the situation and decide how to proceed. "But it was very calm," says Scott.

As the crowd walked on, a school bus painted in brilliant colors arrived on the scene. Music blared from speakers mounted on the bus, and the people, still moving toward their destination, began to sing. Scott says, "There must have been more than five thousand people at this point." The sight and sounds of the moment transfixed him, and he asked Felix to translate the words of the song.

These survivors, most of whom had likely gone days without eating, most of whom had lost friends and family and had been left without homes, kept moving forward, and as they went, they sang, "Jesus will show me the way."

In later taskings, Pathfinders distributed thousands of stuffed animals, along with food rations, to orphans in remote villages. Photo credit: Colonel Dave Larivee

That kind of faith—a faith that inspires hope and renews strength—is at the heart of the work Scott and the Eagles Wings Foundation continue to do in response to some of the world's most devastating disasters. When they are called, that faith allows the Pathfinders to answer, and in doing so, Scott and his fellow volunteers become the instruments of much-needed miracles.

Riccardo Crespo

New Orleans, Louisiana

Hurricane Katrina

I was attending Jazz Fest 2014 with my good friends Clyde and Lorraine Berger, who I first met during a "Continuity Cares" rebuilding effort in New Orleans in 2007, when they told me about a local musician they'd met named Riccardo Crespo and his inspiring story. He and I must've been destined to meet because he just happened to be playing at the same hotel where the Bergers were staying, so they took me to meet him and to hear him play that evening.

Clyde became acquainted with Riccardo while volunteering with Habitat for Humanity in Musician's Village after Hurricane Katrina. When Clyde shared some of Riccardo's story with me, I knew I had to include this activist, community advocate, and hero in my book.

Riccardo's actions demonstrate the resilience disaster survivors can muster when circumstances demand it. He shows us how the perseverance and determination of one person can pay off for an entire community.

Dry, irritated eyes, inexplicable headaches, unrelenting nasal congestion, a cough that wouldn't go away—something was making the residents of Musicians' Village, in New Orleans, Louisiana, sick. At the same time, strange things were happening in their houses. Brand new air conditioning units and microwaves quit working. Light bulbs exploded. Copper wiring and metal fixtures corroded. In 2009, the neighborhood built to provide housing for musicians displaced by Hurricane Katrina seemed to have left the disaster survivors with a new set of problems.

"There is no hurricane that can wash away the music from New Orleans," says Brazilian-born musician Riccardo Crespo. After shutting down his conventional business ventures to dedicate himself to a full-time music career, Riccardo landed in New Orleans in 1999, in the middle of the city's famed Jazz and Heritage Festival. He recalls, "I thought to myself, in a couple of years I'll be performing there. If I'm not performing here in Jazz Fest [by then], I'll leave to Brazil."

The musician immediately connected to the Birthplace of Jazz, partly because the city has a lot in common with his mother country. Along with similar climates, both cultures were born of the blending of European, African, and indigenous art, cuisines, languages, and religious practices. Riccardo's experience in Europe in the early 1980s had taught him that playing his music on the city streets was a sure way to prove himself to an unfamiliar audience. He launched his career in the United States the same way.

Singing and playing guitar, writing, composing, and recording his albums, Riccardo immersed himself in the deeply rooted music community of New Orleans. In 2001, right on track with the goal he'd set for himself, he was invited to play at Jazz Fest for the first time. On stage, he shared his own unique musical style, which he describes as a blend of Música Popular Brasileira, folk, bossa nova, and Latin Jazz. Over the next six years, his music also took on some of the flavor of the city. Riccardo had found a new home.

But in August of 2005, everything changed. Summers in New Orleans are tough for anyone in the tourist industry, including performers. Hot and humid from May to September, the city is largely empty of visitors, and when the hotel where Riccardo was playing let him go for the season, he traveled to Scandinavia. He enjoyed the people of that region, and they embraced his music.

Riccardo intended to return to Louisiana at the end of August, but in Norway he crossed paths with Brazilian friends. Together, they decided to throw a Brazilian Independence Day party on September 7th, so Riccardo postponed his departure. The decision would work out in his favor. The same day he was originally scheduled to fly back to New Orleans, Hurricane Katrina pummeled the city. Riccardo says, "If I had come back, I would not land in New Orleans because my plane would arrive together with Katrina."

Eight thousand miles away, he followed reports of the rising death toll and watched footage of the hurricane, which made landfall with winds up to 140 miles per hour, flooded streets, and people rescued by boat and helicopter. Riccardo was grateful to have avoided the disaster, but he also realized he'd likely lost most of what he owned. Later, he learned his home was under seven feet of water. "But I was lucky," says Riccardo, "because my compositions were on the second floor of my former girlfriend's [place], in the French Quarter, and the roof was damaged, but . . . my compositions were saved. What was left for me was some clothes, my guitar, my harmonicas, and then my music."

As the days passed, he took solace in the fact that his losses were only material. Though he'd dealt with an ongoing health issue throughout that year, he was strong enough to start from near zero. He had to move on with his life. "Not easy," he says, "but not the end of the world."

"Not easy" may be something of an understatement. Much of

New Orleans remained closed to residents, and after playing a final concert in Norway in early September, Riccardo needed a place to go. The cost of living in Oslo was just too expensive for a man in his predicament, so he moved on to Spain, where he had friends. "I slept in twenty different kinds of rooms," he says. "I slept in the car. I slept in the tent, hotel, friends' houses. My goodness, it was a really hard time." Riccardo survived on his talent, playing whatever gigs he could pick up. In November, three months after the hurricane hit the Gulf Coast, he was ready to return to Louisiana and see for himself what his options were for starting over.

Back in New Orleans, Riccardo felt a pronounced shift in the spirit of the city. "It was so heavy energy," he recalls. "So many people died there." Public services hadn't yet been restored, and many neighborhoods were still uninhabitable. After struggling to stay afloat in Europe and finding his adopted home in a worse state than he'd imagined, Riccardo needed to recharge. He headed back to Brazil, where he spent some time on his family's farm, reconnecting to the land and the people of Porto Alegre, in Rio Grande do Sul, and contemplating what his next move should be.

In April of 2006, driven by a growing desire to be a part of the rebuilding and healing of the city, and certain that all signs were directing him to take a leap of faith, Riccardo made his decision. He explains, "I felt that if I would have not come back to New Orleans, I would have been very ungrateful to the city."

During his first week back, Riccardo noticed posters soliciting musicians to apply to buy a new house through the non-profit Habitat for Humanity. World-renowned musical artists and Louisiana natives Harry Connick Jr. and Branford Marsalis had partnered with New Orleans Habitat to develop a neighborhood committed to preserving the musical legacy of the city. It would provide affordable housing for musicians. In addition to seventy-nine single family homes and five duplexes for seniors, the neighborhood would include a small park and a performance venue.

Buying a home in the new development wasn't as simple as calling a real estate agent and choosing a lot. Applicants had to demonstrate credit worthiness, prove they were working musicians who'd been displaced by the disaster, and commit to participating in the construction. Habitat approved Riccardo's application, and in June of 2006, builders broke ground on his new house. Eight months later, he became a resident of Musicians' Village, a collection of shotgun-style houses built with deep front porches and painted in vibrant colors reminiscent of the Caribbean.

It should've been a happy ending, but almost as soon as he moved in, Riccardo began to suffer from dry, itchy eyes. As the months passed, he could find no relief, and other strange things happened. A silver necklace he'd owned for years tarnished and corroded, and no matter how many times he cleaned it, it turned black again. In 2009, stories about tainted drywall distributed to Habitat for Humanity hit the news, and by 2010, Riccardo suspected he might be living in a toxic house. He went looking for answers.

Initially, Habitat for Humanity officials denied any of the banned drywall had been used in Musicians' Village. But Riccardo insisted something was gravely wrong, and the organization finally relented and agreed to run tests. The results were negative. No, Riccardo, was told, his home wasn't built with the Chinese drywall contaminated with high levels of sulfur and heavy metals. As far as the experts were concerned, the building materials had nothing to do with the illnesses and home construction issues popping up in the neighborhood.

But eighteen months later, their symptoms persisting, each of the residents of Musicians' Village received a letter from a journalist investigating the drywall story. The reporter warned that the testing methods Habitat used weren't reliable. Chances were still good that residents were being exposed to toxins. The same day he received the letter, Riccardo called Habitat and requested they retest his home. When the organization's personnel failed to provide a satisfactory response, he went to their office in person.

Habitat's management continued to deny that any contaminated drywall could have found its way into the new neighborhood. However, Riccardo wasn't so easily persuaded, and when they finally gave in and returned to his house, there was no more denying the problem. Riccardo produced proof that his home had been built with the dangerous product. Plainly stamped on the drywall inside the housing for his air conditioning unit were the words "Made in China," along with verbiage specifically used by the manufacturer in question.

Property managers were shocked by the musician's discovery. After all, they'd already tested his home. But when a more rigorous analysis was done, it proved positive for contamination. Riccardo spread the word about these latest results and urged his neighbors to have their homes tested or retested. In the ensuing months, Habitat for Humanity officials learned the distributor had mixed contaminated Chinese product with approved building materials. More than half of the homes of Musicians' Village, and dozens of other houses constructed by the organization after the hurricane, contained the toxic drywall. An organization dedicated to providing housing for those who might otherwise never have an opportunity to realize the American dream of home ownership had built "sick" buildings for people to live in. But Riccardo says, "They were really willing to fix what was wrong."

Throughout the process, Riccardo represented his neighbors' interests in negotiating with the responsible parties. In the end, Habitat for Humanity brought in contractors who removed the bad drywall and damaged wiring and completely renovated the contaminated homes. "They kept the siding, the frame, and the roof," Riccardo recalls. "The rest was changed."

When asked if his neighbors felt lucky to have benefited from his tenacity, Riccardo says simply, "I did what I had to do, you know?" He credits his heritage as a gaucho from South Brazil, a people known for their activism and pioneering spirit, for his persistence in working to resolve the problem.

Hundreds of lawsuits were filed against the drywall manufacturer, and Riccardo was called as a principal witness in one of those cases. "It was a situation I was never in before," he explains. "There [were] five lawyers on one table to my right side, five lawyers at another table to my left side, three cameras filming, like one hundred twenty questions for me to answer."

Because of Riccardo's determination, the collective voice of his neighbors was heard and their concerns answered. Finally, this group of hurricane survivors could rest assured that they came home to what most people take for granted—a house that wasn't making them sick, a safe space. Riccardo continues to reside in Musicians' Village and gives up to 150 performances a year throughout New Orleans, including playing as a featured artist at the festival he first fell in love with. And in March of 2014, the gaucho musical artist, a hero to the people who call Musicians' Village home, became an American citizen.

About the Author

Suzanne is an award-winning and internationally-recognized emergency management and business continuity consultant, instructor and speaker, who has helped governments, communities and companies plan for and respond to disasters for nearly two decades. Her company, SB Crisis Consulting, was recently awarded the global 2015 Innovation & Excellence Award – Excellence in Emergency Management (Canada), as well as both the 2015 and 2014 International Business Excellence Award – Crisis Communications Consultant of the Year (Canada).

Throughout her career, Suzanne has been personally involved in responding to crises such as the 1998 ice storm in Eastern Canada, the 2003 Northeast Blackout, Hurricane Katrina, Hurricane Sandy, as well as numerous floods, fires, severe storms and reputational crises. In recognition of her response work during the 1998 "Ice Storm of the Century" in Canada, she received the Amethyst Award for Outstanding Achievement on behalf of the Government of Ontario.

Prior to her career in emergency management and business continuity, Suzanne was a news reporter and anchor, as well as government press secretary/communications advisor and speechwriter.

In her spare time, Suzanne directs and performs in various community theatre productions in Toronto, and is an active "voluntourist" who has helped respond and rebuild following both Hurricane Katrina and Hurricane Sandy.

For speaking engagements/author events or consulting inquiries, contact Suzanne at:

Suzanne@sbcrisisconsulting.com

1-866-577-7373, ext. 101

www.sbcrisisonsulting.com

@sbcrisis

SBCRISIS**CONSULTING**

Visit www.sbcrisisconsulting.com for more on Suzanne's background, upcoming speaking engagements, recent articles, photo gallery, and much more!

Customized Training and Consulting Services

SB Crisis Consulting, owned and operated by Suzanne Bernier, CEM, CBCP, MBCI, is a boutique crisis management consulting firm that works with governments, communities and companies to help plan for and respond to disasters.

Consulting services include the development, review, testing/exercising and enhancement of:

- Business Continuity Plans/Programs
- Emergency Response Plans
- Crisis Communications Plans
- Infectious Disease Outbreak/Epidemic/Pandemic Plans

Exercise development, delivery and evaluation services for various scenarios, including:

- Flood, fire, severe storm, extended power outage emergencies
- Infectious disease outbreaks
- Reputational crises
- Active shooter/armed intruder incidents

Instruction/Training Course Development and Delivery:

- Crisis Communications for Professionals
- Communicating in a Crisis
- Spokesperson/Media Training
- Emergency Management Basics
- Hazard Identification and Risk Assessment
- Emergency Operations Center (EOC) Management
- Incident Management System (IMS)
- Customized Curriculum Development and Delivery

Speaking services:

- Keynote presentations
- Conference breakout sessions
- Panels
- Seminars
- Lunch and Learn sessions
- Webinars
- University lectures
- Corporate functions

For more information, see the Services section at www.sbcrisisconsulting.com